ExpressWays

COMPANION WORKBOOK

2A

Steven J. Molinsky · Bill Bliss

Contributing Author
Ann Kennedy

Prentice Hall Regents, Englewood Cliffs, NJ 07632

Editorial/production supervision and
 interior design: Tünde A. Dewey
Development: Bill Preston
Cover design: Lundgren Graphics, Ltd.
Manufacturing buyer: Laura Crossland

Cover drawing by Gabriel Polonsky

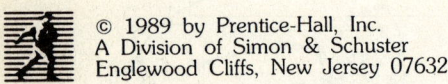
© 1989 by Prentice-Hall, Inc.
A Division of Simon & Schuster
Englewood Cliffs, New Jersey 07632

All rights reserved. No part of this book may be
reproduced, in any form or by any means,
without permission in writing from the publisher.

Printed in the United States of America

10 9 8 7 6 5 4 3 2 1

ISBN 0-13-298308-7

Prentice-Hall International (UK) Limited, *London*
Prentice-Hall of Australia Pty. Limited, *Sydney*
Prentice-Hall Canada Inc., *Toronto*
Prentice-Hall Hispanoamericana, S.A., *Mexico*
Prentice-Hall of India Private Limited, *New Delhi*
Prentice-Hall of Japan, Inc., *Tokyo*
Simon & Schuster Asia Pte. Ltd., *Singapore*
Editora Prentice-Hall do Brasil, Ltda., *Rio de Janeiro*

CONTENTS

Chapter 1	1
Chapter 2	11
Chapter 3	18
Check-Up Test	28
Chapter 4	30
Chapter 5	39
Chapter 6	50
Check-Up Test	60
Chapter 7	62
Chapter 8	70
Chapter 9	84
Check-Up Test	95
Tape Scripts for Listening Exercises	98

1

A. WHO, WHAT, WHEN, ... Student Course Book p. 2

| Who | What | When | Where | Which | Why | How |

1. __Where__ do you live?
   On the fifth floor.

2. _____ is he?
   He's my new neighbor.

3. _____ bank do you go to?
   The Empire Bank.

4. _____ are Frank and Susan?
   Fine.

5. _____ did you meet her?
   Yesterday.

6. _____ are you majoring in English?
   I like it.

7. _____ did they steal?
   A car.

8. _____ is from Greece?
   George.

B. WHICH APARTMENT ARE WE GOING TO? Student Course Book p. 2

| Am I ? | Is { he / she / it } ? | Are { we / you / they } ? | Do { I / you / we / they } ? | Does { he / she / it } ? |

1. Which apartment __are__ we going to?

2. Where _____ you live?

3. Why _____ I here?

4. What _____ you majoring in?

5. _____ Diane live on the second floor?

6. Who _____ she?

7. When _____ he going to move in?

8. _____ they from Guatemala?

9. _____ this your car?

10. How _____ you do?

C. MR. REED'S CLASS

Student Course Book p. 3

Fill in the blanks.

1. Excuse me. __Is__ this Room 15?

    Yes, it _____. _____ you looking for Mr. Reed's class?

    Yes, I _____.

2. _____ Mr. Reed give a lot of homework?

    Yes, he _____, and his tests _____ very hard.

    How _____ you know that?

3. Mr. Reed _____ late today.
    What time is it?
    10:15.

    _____ you think Mr. Reed _____ going to come to class today?

    Yes, I _____.

D. LISTENING

Student Course Book p. 3

Listen and circle the correct response.

1. My brother.
   (At the bank.)

2. Diane Frank.
   Fine.

3. To the 2nd floor.
   Last week.

4. In my car.
   To my apartment.

5. She's my wife.
   She's fine.

6. 103.
   Last week.

7. And you?
   English.

8. I am.
   Nice meeting you.

9. Hello.
   And you?

E. MORE QUESTIONS

Student Course Book p. 3

1. [What / Where] city are you from? *(What circled)*
2. [Who / Which] class are you in?
3. [How / Whose] homework is this?
4. [When / Who] did you start studying?
5. [Whose / Who] is your new neighbor?
6. [Who / How] did you meet her?
7. [Which / When] department did you work in?
8. [Where / What] did you live in Greece?
9. [Who / Whose] apartment did they rob?
10. [What / How] did you enjoy your new class?

F. WHERE DO YOU WORK?

Student Course Book p. 3

> Where **do** you work?   How **are** you enjoy**ing** it?   When **did** you start?
> I work in Personnel.   I**'m** enjoy**ing** it very much.   I start**ed** yesterday.

1. Who ___did___ you talk to?
   I talked to my supervisor.
2. Where _____ you live?
   In the city.
3. Where _____ you going?
   To the bank.
4. When _____ you start studying English?
   Several years ago.
5. What _____ you do here?
   I work in Accounting.
6. _____ you enjoying your classes?
   Yes. Very much.

3

G. MATCHING

Student Course Book p. 3

Draw a line to the correct response for each group.

1. What floor is your class on?   Last week.
2. When did you write to her?   I don't think so.
3. Do you have to work this weekend?   The second.

4. Where does he come from?   Yes. In Tokyo.
5. Who do they work for?   Mr. Bell.
6. Is Mary living in Japan?   Japan.

7. Whose car is this?   Mr. Frank.
8. How's your new car?   Steve's.
9. Who's working here tonight?   Fantastic!

H. HE STARTED YESTERDAY

Student Course Book p. 3

1. When did he start working?

   He started working yesterday.

2. Where are they from?

   _____ Ethiopia.

3. How is she enjoying her new job?

   _____ it very much.

4. Whose car did they steal?

   _____ the Bensons' car.

5. Which class do you enjoy?

   _____ English.

6. What country are they moving to?

   _____ Japan.

7. Where did Jimmy live last year?

   _____ in Detroit.

8. When do you work?

   _____ on weekends.

I. FAMILY

Student Course Book p. 4

Find the following words and put a circle around them.
You will find them in two directions: *down* and *across*.

brother
father
sister
wife
daughter
husband
mother
sons

```
k o l t f s m a u i s
c v b o u y o f r d b
w i p q f a t h e r t
d a r i t e h t o e o
f a s m i l e s i s t
(b r o t h e r) o c t h
f o n o u m o s i w f
b r s i s t e r o i t
a d o t b e r g r f e
s u t d a u g h t e r
m o f s n g l t s o s
w i n o d a i o m o g
```

J. MORE MATCHING

Student Course Book p. 4

Draw a line to the correct response for each group.

1. Hello.
2. How are you doing?
3. Nice meeting you.

It's nice meeting you, too.
How do you do?
Fine.

4. You're new here, aren't you?
5. How are you?
6. Where do you work?

The second floor.
All right.
Yes, I am.

7. This is Philip.
8. How are things?
9. Are you new here?

Yes, I am.
Nice meeting you.
Okay, thanks.

K. WHICH WORDS ARE CORRECT?

Student Course Book p. 4

1. How are you [things / (doing)] ?

2. This is [myself / my wife] .

3. I'd like to [introduce / meet] myself.

4. I'm [thank you / all right] .

5. I'd like to [introduce / meet] you to Carl.

6. I'm glad to [meeting / meet] you.

L. COUNTRIES

Student Course Book p. 5

1. [Spain   Spanish   Barcelona]

____Spain____ is a beautiful country.

Yes, it is. _____ is one of my favorite cities.

Do you speak _____ well?
Yes, I do.

2. [Japan   Japanese   Tokyo]

_____ is my favorite city in _____.

I agree. What's your favorite _____ food?
Sushi.

3. [Italy   Italians   Italian]

A lot of _____ go on vacation in August.

That's right. I went to _____ to study _____ last August and there weren't a lot of people in Rome!

M. ARE YOU SURPRISED?

Student Course Book p. 5

1. __Are__ you surprised?
   Yes, __I am__.

2. Where _____ you work?
   _____ at the bank.

3. _____ a lot of people visit Stockholm in January?
   No, _____.

4. _____ this your passport?
   Yes, _____.

5. When _____ they want to go on vacation?
   _____ to go on vacation in July.

6. What part of Brazil _____ he from?
   _____ from Rio de Janeiro.

7. How long _____ she plan to visit?
   _____ to visit for six days.

Where **are** you from?	**Are** you from Italy?
I'm from Italy.	Yes, I **am**.
	No, I'm **not**.
Where **do** you live?	**Do** you live in Rome?
I live in Rome.	Yes, I **do**.
	No, I **don't**.

8. _____ he speak Japanese well?
   No, _____.

9. Where _____ they going?
   _____ going to Seoul.

10. _____ they have their passports?
    Yes, _____.

11. Where _____ you plan to go?
    _____ to go to Barcelona.

12. _____ you going on vacation soon?
    No, _____.

N. ARE YOU AMERICAN?

Student Course Book p. 5

1. __Are you__ American?
   No, I'm not. I'm Canadian.

2. _____ in Mexico City?
   No. He lives in Acapulco.

3. _____ doing?
   She's fine.

4. _____ live in?
   They live in Apartment 302.

5. _____ she from?
   She's from London.

6. _____ here on business?
   No, they aren't. They're here on vacation.

7. _____ Korea?
   Yes, we are. We're from Seoul.

8. _____?
   The school year ends in June.

9. _____?
   They speak English and Japanese.

10. _____?
    I plan to visit for about two weeks.

O. WHICH WORD?

Student Course Book p. 6

1. I'd like to charge my [check / **(bill)**]

2. I [requested / traveled] a regular room.

3. Is the suite [facing / in] the park?

4. Could you please [name / spell] that?

5. That's [right / actually not]

6. Do you have a [reservation / information]?

7. Are you traveling with your [bellhop / wife]?

8. We have the correct [problem / information]

9. Here's my American Express [computer / card]

10. I'd like a [size / twin] bed.

P. WE HAD THE WRONG INFORMATION

Student Course Book p. 6

1. I think we [**(had)** / are having] the wrong information.

2. The bellhop [will take / took] your luggage to your room in a few minutes.

3. I understand you [made / are making] your reservation last weekend.

4. How many nights [do you stay / are you staying]?

5. I see you [have / make] a reservation.

6. I guess we [make / made] a mistake.

Q. LITTLE WORDS Student Course Book p. 6

| does | do | is |

1. __Is__ this information wrong?
2. _____ you spell that with an "E"?
3. What _____ that mean?

| did | are | does |

4. _____ you request a suite?
5. Where _____ the bellhops?
6. _____ he want to pay by check?

| is | are | does |

7. Where _____ you going to stay?
8. _____ he traveling alone?
9. _____ the hotel have his reservation on the computer?

| are | do | does |

10. _____ the suite face the park?
11. How long _____ you staying?
12. _____ you have the correct information now?

R. WRONG INFORMATION Student Course Book p. 6

Circle the letter of the correct response.

1. I see here your first name is Jim.
   a. Actually, no. It's Tim. *(circled)*
   b. Sure.
   c. I guess you just have the wrong information.

2. I see here you asked for a suite.
   a. No. I want a jacket.
   b. Not really. I requested a regular room.
   c. No, thank you.

3. I see here you're paying by check.
   a. No problem.
   b. Thank you.
   c. No, actually not. I have my credit card.

4. I see here you want to stay four nights.
   a. No, not really.
   b. Oh. No problem.
   c. All right.

5. I see here you're paying by check.
   a. Could you please spell that?
   b. Not really. I'm charging it.
   c. Thank you.

S. NUMBERS Student Course Book p. 6

Draw a line to the correct number.

1. social security number — 05/04/68
2. date of birth — 312-60-7843
3. telephone number — 3327G
4. I.D. number — (904) 544-7956

T. PERSONNEL OFFICE Student Course Book p. 7

Complete the missing lines in the following conversation with appropriate questions. Use complete sentences. Then practice the conversation.

May I help you?

    Yes. Is this the Personnel Office?

Yes, it is.

    I'm a new employee.

What's your name? 1

    George Frankel.

Nice to meet you. Let me fill out this "New Employee Form."

_____ 2

    F-R-A-N-K-E-L.

_____ 3

    694 Crane Drive.

_____ 4

    559-7854.

_____ 5

    My social security number is 503-78-8468.

_____ 6

    July 30, 1967.

_____ 7

    No. I don't have medical insurance.

_____ 8

    My supervisor's name is Mrs. Wilson.

Okay. Thank you very much, Mr. Frankel. I'm glad you're working with us.

    I am, too.

U. READING: *No More Numbers, Please!*   Student Course Book p. 7

    Maria came to the United States from Spain two days ago. She's staying with her brother and his family all summer because she wants to study English at the local university.

    Maria had to fill out a long form at the university. She was very surprised because she had to remember so many numbers! She wrote her brother's address with the zip code and apartment number, her new telephone number and area code, her passport number, and her brother's office telephone number. The form also asked for a social security number and a medical insurance I.D. number, but she didn't have these.

    Maria gave the form to the secretary in the English department. The secretary took the form and said, "Write this number down. Don't forget it. It's your student I.D. number and it's very important. Please put this number on your check when you pay your tuition and put it under your name when you take tests. You'll also need this number to take books out of the library." Another number to remember! Maria wrote the long number down: 90X31058.

    Maria had a headache and wanted to go home. She remembered that the Number 93 bus came at 10:11. Or was it the Number 39 at 11:10? Oh, no! Too many new numbers!

I. TRUE or FALSE? Put a T if the sentence is true, and an F if it is false.

____ 1. Maria wanted to study English.

____ 2. Maria's brother and his family live in Spain.

____ 3. A zip code is part of a telephone number.

____ 4. 90X31058 is Maria's new medical insurance number.

____ 5. Maria didn't remember the number of her bus.

II. DID YOU UNDERSTAND? Put a circle around the letter of the correct answer.

1. Maria is
    a. a secretary.
    b. a student.
    c. English.

2. Maria is going to study
    a. during the summer.
    b. Spanish.
    c. her social security number.

3. She's staying
    a. at the university.
    b. in Spain.
    c. with her brother.

4. On the form, Maria wrote
    a. her address in Spain.
    b. her office telephone number.
    c. her address in the United States.

5. She also wrote
    a. her social security number.
    b. her passport number.
    c. her medical insurance number.

6. The number 90X31058 is
    a. her social security number.
    b. her student I.D. number.
    c. the bus number.

7. Maria had a headache because
    a. she wanted to go home.
    b. she remembered that the Number 93 bus comes at 10:11.
    c. she had to remember too many new numbers.

2

A. WHAT'S NEW?   Student Course Book p. 10

| get-got   win-won   find-found   write-wrote   leave-left |

1. What's happening?

   I __left__ my keys in the house. Now I can't get in.

2. What's new with you?

   My husband just _____ a raise.

3. So what's new?

   We finally _____ a nice apartment.

4. What's happening with you?

   We just _____ a very big check for our new house.

5. So what's new with you?

   My son _____ the lottery last week.

6. So what's happening?

   Timmy _____ his lunch at home. I have to take it to him.

B. I WON FIRST PRIZE!   Student Course Book p. 10

1. Did you win?

   Yes. I __won__ first prize!

2. Did they have apple pie?

   No. They _____ ice cream.

3. Did she finally find an apartment?

   Yes. She _____ it yesterday.

4. Did John meet the Wilsons in apartment 3G?

   No, but he _____ the Bensons in apartment 3A.

5. Did you write to your sister?

   Yes. I _____ to her yesterday.

6. Did Mary get a new job in Personnel?

   No, but she _____ a raise.

C. HE DIDN'T GET A RAISE   Student Course Book p. 11

1. He got a new job, but he __didn't get__ a raise.

2. She found her house keys, but she _____ _____ her car keys.

3. We met Sally, but we _____ _____ her parents.

4. I had some apple pie, but I _____ _____ any ice cream.

5. They won a prize, but they _____ _____ first prize.

D. I'D LIKE YOU TO MEET MY FIANCÉ

Student Course Book p. 11

	I - my	We - our
	He - his	You - your
	She - her	They - their
	It - its	

1. I'd like you to meet [our / (my)] fiancé.

2. He got the raise [his / he] was hoping for.

3. Did Tom get [their / his] paycheck?

4. She met them on [her / my] way to work.

5. [They're / Their] very busy right now.

6. Is [its / it] Valentine's Day today?

7. [Our / We] friends moved away last month.

8. [He / Her] didn't receive a prize.

9. What's new with [your / you]?

10. [Her / She] was away on vacation last week.

11. What happened while [I / I'm] was away?

12. [We / Our] broke up last night.

13. They wrecked [they / their] new car!

14. What's [you / your] name?

15. Poor dog! [It's / Its] leg is broken.

E. LISTENING

Student Course Book p. 11

Listen to the sentence. Circle the correct response.

1. (That's great!) / That's a shame!

2. That's fantastic! / What a shame!

3. That's wonderful! / I'm sorry to hear that.

4. That's too bad! / Congratulations!

5. What a shame! / That's wonderful!

6. I'm very sorry. / That's great!

7. I'm so sorry. / That's fantastic!

8. That's a shame! / That's wonderful!

9. That's great! / That's too bad!

F. WHERE DID YOU HEAR THAT?

Student Course Book pp. 12–13

Fill in the blank to complete the question.

1. <u>Is Bill going to move to</u> California?
   No. Bill is going to move to Nevada.

2. _____ last weekend?
   No. They got married last month.

3. _____ the day shift?
   No. The boss plans to lay off the night shift.

4. _____ on strike?
   No. The teachers aren't going to go on strike.

5. _____ quit?
   No. Alice wants to take a vacation.

6. _____ our apartment building?
   No. The Trump Corporation bought the building across the street.

7. _____ take a cut in pay?
   No. The secretaries are going to have to shorten their breaks.

8. _____ cancel our final exam?
   No. Miss Anderson wants to change the date of the exam.

9. _____ at the union meeting last night?
   No. Our supervisor was at another meeting last night.

10. _____ in the cafeteria?
    No. They're eating lunch in the park.

G. RUMORS

Student Course Book pp. 12–13

Fill in the blank.

1. They were talking about it in the elevator. <u>They weren't talking</u> about it in the hallway.

2. Fred didn't tell me. The boss _____<u>told</u>_____ me.

3. I heard it from Debbie. I _____ it from Rita.

4. Alice is talking about her gym teacher. She _____ about her English teacher.

5. She didn't mention it at the meeting. She _____ it at lunch.

6. We're going to have to shorten our lunch breaks. We _____ have to take a cut in pay.

7. It isn't true. _____ just a rumor.

8. The boss wants him to quit. The boss _____ to fire him.

9. She didn't get married to Tom. She _____ married to Jim.

H. WHEN WILL YOU . . . ? Student Course Book p. 14

	I'll	
	He'll	
	She'll	} visit some friends.
	We'll	
	You'll	
	They'll	

1. When will you finish your chores?
   I'll finish my chores by noon.

2. When will your husband get a promotion?
   _____ next year.

3. When will the workers go on strike?
   _____ at midnight.

4. When will Marsha do her Christmas shopping?
   _____ on December 24.

5. When will you tell Bobby the good news?
   _____ when he gets home.

6. When will we have to take a cut in pay?
   _____ next month.

I. WHEN ARE YOU GOING TO . . . ? Student Course Book p. 14

	I'm	
	He's	
	She's	} going to finish my term paper.
	We're	
	You're	
	They're	

1. When are you going to finish your term paper?
   I'm going to finish my term paper this weekend.

2. When is your son going to take his driver's test?
   _____ tomorrow afternoon.

3. When are you and your wife going to visit your new grandson?
   _____ next week.

4. When am I going to get my raise?
   _____ very soon.

5. When is your mother going to take us to the circus?
   _____ on Saturday.

J. I'LL TAKE THEM TO THE CIRCUS

Student Course Book p. 14

1. Where will you take the children on Sunday?

   _____ I'll take _____ them to the circus.

2. Why is Judy going to move out of her apartment?

   _____ because she and Joe are getting a divorce.

3. How many people will Alice probably invite to the party?

   _____ about twenty people.

4. When will Mr. Rutherford have the next meeting?

   _____ it when he gets back from vacation.

5. What room will you paint next?

   _____ the bathroom.

6. When are you and I going to get married?

   _____ when you get a good job.

7. Where will you and your husband be next weekend?

   _____ at the beach on vacation.

K. I SUPPOSE SO

Student Course Book p. 15

Draw a line to the correct words for each group.

1. I suppose ⎯⎯⎯⎯⎯⎯⎯⎯⎯⎯⎯⎯⎯ positive.
2. I don't know ⎯⎯⎯⎯⎯⎯⎯⎯⎯⎯ so.
3. I'm not   for sure.

4. What are you   shame!
5. What a   plans?
6. What are your   doing?

7. Is anything the   wrong?
8. What's   you?
9. Who told   matter?

15

L. WHERE ARE THEY GOING?

Student Course Book p. 15

Fill in the blank with the correct word.

1. __Where__ are they going?
   To a birthday party.

2. _____ are they going?
   This afternoon.

3. _____ birthday is it?
   Bobby's.

4. _____ did he get?
   A speeding ticket.

5. _____ did it happen?
   On Garden Avenue.

6. _____ was the ticket?
   Thirty dollars.

7. _____ is she going to quit?
   Because she got a new job.

8. _____ is she going to leave?
   Next week.

9. _____ is she going to work?
   At the Davis Corporation.

10. _____ do you do your shopping?
    On Saturday afternoons.

11. _____ goes with you?
    My husband.

12. _____ do you go?
    To the new shopping mall.

M. LISTENING

Student Course Book p. 15

Listen to the conversation. Circle the letter of the correct sentence.

1.
   a. She's from Los Angeles.
   (b.) She's from Denver.

2.
   a. His name is Jim.
   b. He teaches gym.

3.
   a. They'll get more money.
   b. They're going to have rice.

4.
   a. He's going to take the test.
   b. He took the test.

5.
   a. They're going to go on strike.
   b. They went on strike.

6.
   a. They aren't sure about Fred.
   b. Fred is going to go far away.

7.
   a. They're in Cleveland.
   b. She went to college in Cleveland.

8.
   a. He's originally from New York.
   b. He went to college in New York.

9.
   a. He wrote for a newspaper.
   b. He taught English.

10.
    a. She has only one child.
    b. She has a son and a daughter.

N. READING: *The Weekend* Student Course Book p. 15

Many people in the United States look forward to the weekend. It's the time to relax, have fun, and do things around the house.

On Friday nights, many people like to relax after work. They go out for dinner, to the movies, concerts, or plays. Other people just like to stay home and watch TV.

On Saturday mornings, supermarkets and shopping malls are crowded with people buying food, clothing, presents, and other things they need.

Many people do chores around the house on Saturday afternoons. They paint, clean attics and basements, rake leaves, do laundry, and wash cars.

On Saturday evenings, many people like to go out. They visit friends, invite people to come over for dinner, or go to the movies, the theater, or a sporting event.

On Sunday mornings, many people like to sleep late, especially people who stayed up late on Saturday night. People often go to church on Sunday. They read the newspaper, and often eat a late breakfast called "brunch."

On Sunday afternoons when the weather is nice, you see many families at the zoo or in parks. During the winter, many people spend Sunday afternoons at theaters, museums, or shopping malls. Many families have a big dinner on Sunday afternoons. Grandparents and other relatives often come to visit. On Sunday evenings, people usually stay home and prepare for the week ahead.

Weekends can be very busy!

I. TRUE or FALSE? Put a T if the sentence is true, and an F if it is false.

____ 1. Weekends begin on Saturday afternoons.

____ 2. People usually relax on Saturday mornings and afternoons.

____ 3. There are usually a lot of parties on Sunday nights.

____ 4. People probably eat "brunch" at around 11:00 in the morning.

____ 5. The zoo is probably crowded on beautiful Sunday afternoons.

II. DO YOU UNDERSTAND? Circle the letter of the correct answer.

1. People relax, have fun, and do chores
    a. on Friday nights.
    b. during the weekends.
    c. on Saturday evenings.

2. Most Americans do their shopping
    a. on Friday evenings.
    b. on Sunday mornings.
    c. on Saturdays.

3. People usually spend Sunday afternoons inside
    a. when the weather is cold.
    b. during the summer months.
    c. and eat "brunch."

4. Most people look forward to the weekend because
    a. everybody goes shopping during the weekend.
    b. they don't have to go to their jobs.
    c. they are very busy.

5. People probably go to bed early on
    a. Friday nights.
    b. Saturday nights.
    c. Sunday nights.

3

A. DIRECTORY ASSISTANCE
Student Course Book p. 18

Unscramble the questions. Then practice the dialog.

1. (help May you I)

    _____May I help you_____?
    I'd like the number of John Henley.

2. (does live he What city in)

    _____?
    Boston.

3. (his spell you do How name last)

    _____?
    H-E-N-L-E-Y.

4. (you address know Do his)

    _____?
    I think he lives on Kirkland Avenue.

5. (that's spelling sure you the Are correct)

    _____
    _____?
    I'm pretty sure, but I'll check again.

B. WHAT'S THE QUESTION?
Student Course Book p. 18

1. _____Where does_____ Steve live?
   He lives on Madison Street.

2. _____ move?
   They're going to move to Dallas.

3. _____ spell "boulevard"?
   B-O-U-L-E-V-A-R-D.

4. _____ the news?
   My wife told me the news.

5. _____ begin?
   Class begins at 9:00.

6. _____ Korean?
   Yes. They're from Seoul.

7. _____ late?
   She was late because she missed her bus.

8. _____ sure?
   No, I'm not.

9. _____ go to New York?
   We're going to go next weekend.

10. _____ "avenue" mean?
    It means "a big, busy street."

C. LISTENING

Student Course Book p. 18

Listen and complete the sentence.

| living   leaving |

1. a. in Dallas.
   b. right now.

| cars   cards |

2. a. in the envelopes.
   b. in the garage.

| plants   plans |

3. a. in your garden?
   b. for the weekend?

| shop   stop |

4. a. at the red light?
   b. for the groceries?

| walk   work |

5. a. to the store.
   b. until 6:00.

| chicken   kitchen |

6. a. before we cook it.
   b. floor.

| please   peas |

7. a. try again.
   b. are good for you.

| gym   him |

8. a. class?
   b. to the circus?

| who   how |

9. a. to get there?
   b. she is?

D. LISTENING

Student Course Book p. 18

Listen to the conversation. Circle the correct word.

1. You
    (Yu)

2. Flanigan
    Flanagin

3. Beech
    Beach

4. Whittier
    Wittler

5. Krizick
    Krizik

6. Rio di Janiero
    Rio de Janeiro

7. Hanley
    Henley

8. Ramirez
    Ramires

E. NO, IT ISN'T

Student Course Book p. 19

1. Is this 493-6843?

   No, _it isn't_____.

2. Do you have the correct address?

   No, _____.

3. Does Joe know her telephone number?

   No, _____.

4. Are the Smiths from Canada?

   No, _____.

5. Is this Madison Street?

   No, _____.

6. Does Lucy live here?

   No, _____.

7. Am I wrong?

   No, _____.

8. Is Mary a telephone operator?

   No, _____.

9. Do they have a telephone yet?

   No, _____.

10. Are you Mr. Robinson?

    No, _____.

I'm	not.		
He / She / It	isn't.	We / You / They	aren't.

I / We / You / They	don't.	He / She / It	doesn't.

F. NO, THEY DIDN'T

Student Course Book p. 19

1. Did the workers go on strike last night?

   No, _they didn't_____.

2. Was your daughter at school today?

   No, _____.

3. Did you dial the wrong number?

   No, _____.

4. Were Mr. and Mrs. Taylor home last night?

   No, _____.

5. Was that the correct address?

   No, _____.

6. Did Mrs. Taylor have the correct number?

   No, _____.

7. Was your brother there?

   No, _____.

8. Were you late?

   No, _____.

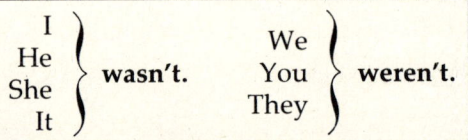

G. LISTENING

Student Course Book p. 19

Listen to the conversation. Circle the correct number.

1. 593-7855 / (539-7899)
2. 952-8622 / 592-8622
3. 832-5600 / 832-5660
4. 860-5439 / 680-3954
5. 438-3593 / 834-5935
6. 648-2341 / 648-2541

H. EXCUSE ME ...

Student Course Book p. 20

Complete the sentences.

1. What time does the train leave for Montreal?

   _____It leaves_____ at 5:45.

2. Does this bus go downtown?

   No. _____ uptown.

3. When does the parking lot close?

   _____ every night at 10:00.

4. What time does the ticket office open?

   _____ at 8:00.

5. Does the express train to New York leave from this platform?

   No. _____ from the other platform.

6. When does the bus from Atlanta arrive?

   _____ at about 3:45.

7. Does the train from Boston stop at this station?

   No. _____ at the station downtown.

I. WHICH WORD IS RIGHT?

Student Course Book p. 20

Circle the correct word.

1. Flight 35 leaves from [(gate) / track] 9.

2. You can get your [plane / track] here.

3. Your ship leaves from [platform / pier] 2.

4. The Number 6 [train / bus] is on track 1.

5. The [monorail / platform] is leaving now.

6. Your [bus / pier] is at gate 13.

7. It goes to the [flight / parking lot].

8. Where can I [go to / get] the A train?

J. WE'VE GOT TO GO!

Student Course Book p. 21

Complete the sentences.

> I've got to
> We've got to
> You've got to } go.
> They've got to
>
> He's got to
> She's got to } go.
> It's got to

1. We can't go to lunch now. _We've got to_ go to a meeting.
2. I can't go shopping now. _____ get to my job interview!
3. My sisters can't come to my wedding. _____ stay in Chicago.
4. Mr. Hendricks can't meet us for lunch. _____ go to a funeral.
5. You have to stay home. _____ finish your homework.
6. It can't be true! _____ be a rumor!
7. Aunt Jane missed her plane. _____ take a later flight.
8. Cathy and I won't be there. _____ go to our graduation.
9. We can't wait for them. _____ go right now.
10. I can't wait. _____ get the next bus.

K. I'VE GOT TO GO

Student Course Book p. 21

Circle the correct words.

> I've got to go. = I have to go.

1. She's [(got to leave) / to leave].
2. We [have to / got to] study.
3. [I / I've] got to go now.
4. It's [got / has got] to leave.
5. Jeff [have got to / has to] go to work.
6. [You / You've] have to purchase a ticket.
7. Do they [have to / have got to] get the next bus?
8. Mary [has / has got to] take the ferry.

L. PARDON ME . . .

Student Course Book p. 21

Complete the missing line of the conversation with an appropriate question.

1. Excuse me. <u>Where is the 7:15 train to Philadelphia</u>?
   The 7:15 train to Philadelphia is on track 5.
   Track 5?
   Right.

2. Pardon me. _____?
   The next flight to Chicago is at 6:30.
   At 6:30?
   That's right.

3. Pardon me. _____?
   You can purchase a ticket right here.
   Right here?
   Yes.

4. Pardon me. _____?
   The next ferry to Manhattan leaves at 7:30.
   Not until 7:30?
   That's right.

5. Excuse me. _____?
   The flight from Detroit is late because it's snowing there.
   It's snowing there?
   Yes.

M. DEPARTURES AND ARRIVALS

Student Course Book p. 21

1. Where can you get the flight to Denver? <u>Gate 15</u>
   When does it leave? <u>7:05 P.M.</u>

2. When will the flight from New York arrive? _____
   Where will you go to meet it? _____

3. What time does the plane leave for Los Angeles? _____
   Where can you get it? _____

4. Where does the 6:15 flight go? _____
   What gate does it leave from? _____

5. Which gate does the next flight to New York leave from? _____
   What time will it leave? _____

6. When will the flight from Boston get here? _____
   Which gate will it arrive at? _____

DEPARTURES

To:	Gate	Departs
Chicago	24	6:15 P.M.
Denver	15	7:05 P.M.
Los Angeles	34	8:30 A.M.
New York	10	3:15 P.M.

ARRIVALS

From:	Gate	Arrives
Boston	11	4:15 P.M.
New York	7	12:35 P.M.
Philadelphia	21	11:10 A.M.

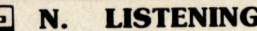 **N. LISTENING**   Student Course Book p. 21

Listen to the announcement.   Circle the words you hear.

1. (Las Vegas) / Los Angeles
2. gate 7 / gate 11
3. 9:30 / 5:30
4. Philadelphia / Broadway
5. gate 45 / gate 17
6. San Francisco / San Fernando
7. 8:02 / 10:30
8. 6:00 / gate 8

O. MATCHING   Student Course Book pp. 22–23

Draw a line to the correct words for each group.

1. Walk ——————————— three blocks to Main Street.
2. Follow ——————————— to the next corner and turn left.
3. Drive about   this road and turn right at the light.

4. Turn left   on the right.
5. You'll see it   onto First Street.
6. Take   the next left.

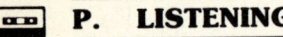 **P. LISTENING**   Student Course Book pp. 22–23

Listen and follow the directions to different places.   Write the letter of the place the people are talking about in each conversation.

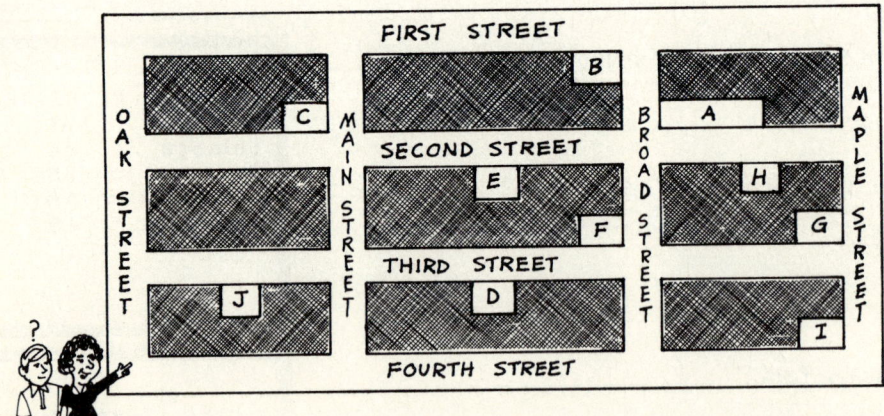

1. __F__   4. _____   7. _____
2. _____   5. _____   8. _____
3. _____   6. _____   9. _____

Q. DIRECTIONS

Student Course Book pp. 22–23

In the space below, draw a map.   Show your school and your home.

Now write the directions from your school to your home.

....
....
....
....
....
....

R. HOW DO YOU SAY IT?

Student Course Book pp. 22–23

Circle the best answer.

1. _____ know how to get to Route 1?
   a. Could you possibly
   b. Are you
   (c.) Do you by any chance

2. Are you _____?
   a. following you
   b. with me
   c. understand

3. Could you _____ again?
   a. please
   b. say that
   c. possibly

4. Now I've _____.
   a. understand
   b. following you
   c. got it

5. Have you _____?
   a. with me so far
   b. got that
   c. possibly repeat that

6. Can you _____?
   a. tell me how to get there
   b. following me so far
   c. know how to get there

7. Now I _____.
   a. understand
   b. didn't get that
   c. with you

8. _____ repeat that?
   a. Do you
   b. Could you possibly
   c. Have you

25

S. LISTENING   Student Course Book pp. 22–23

Listen to the conversation.   Did the person understand the directions?   Circle *Yes* or *No*.

1. (Yes) / No
2. Yes / No
3. Yes / No
4. Yes / No
5. Yes / No
6. Yes / No
7. Yes / No
8. Yes / No

T. LOST!   Student Course Book pp. 22–23

Fill in the blanks.   Then practice the conversation with another student.

Michael!   Where were you?   We started dinner at 8:00.

I apologize, but I (get) _____got_____ lost.
                                            1

What happened?

Well, I (miss) _____ the 7:15 bus, so I (walk) _____
                    2   3

eight blocks to get the subway.   I (get) _____ off the train at Center
                                                 4

Station and (go) _____ down River Street for three blocks.   Then I
                         5

(turn) _____ right.
            6

Oh, no!

Well, I knew that (be) _____ wrong.   I didn't (see) _____
                              7   8

a sign for Oak Street.   I (take) _____ a taxi and I (tell)
                                         9

_____ the driver to drive down Main Street to Oak Street.   Well, he
     10

(drive) _____ in the wrong direction for several miles.   Finally, he (stop)
             11

_____ at a service station and we (look) _____
     12   13

at a map.   We (find) _____ Oak Street on the map right away.
                              14

I can't believe it!   But I'm glad you're here!   Better late than never!   (Be) _____ you
                                                                                                              15

hungry?

U. READING: *Honk! Honk!*

Student Course Book pp. 24–25

Rush hour traffic is a problem in many big cities around the world. Commuters rush to and from their jobs in cars, buses, subways, trains, taxis, and even on bicycles. Large cities in the United States have two rush hours—one in the morning and one in the evening. But in cities in other parts of the world, there are four rush hours. In Athens and Rome, for example, many workers go home for lunch and a nap. After this midday break, they rush back to their jobs and work for a few more hours.

In Tokyo, there's a big rush hour underground. Most of the people in Tokyo take the subways. The trains are very crowded. Subway employees called "packers" wear white gloves and help "pack" the commuters into the trains when the doors close. They make sure that all purses, briefcases, clothes, and hands are inside the trains.

In Seoul, many commuters prefer to take taxis to get to work. To "hail a cab," many people stand at intersections and raise two fingers. This means they'll pay the cab driver double the usual fare. Some people even raise three fingers! They'll pay *three* times the normal rate.

Streets in Rome are very crowded with automobiles and mopeds during rush hours. The city can't make its streets wider and it can't build new highways, because it doesn't want to disturb the many historic sites in the city, such as the Forum and the Colosseum. It took the city fifteen years to construct a new subway system. Construction had to stop every time workers found old artifacts and discovered places of interest to archaeologists.

Athens is another ancient city which cannot build large highways. To deal with rush hour problems, the city government decided to cut traffic in half. Drivers with license plate numbers ending in 0 through 4 can only drive on certain days. Drivers with numbers ending in 5 through 9 can drive on the other days.

In Washington, D.C., there are special lanes on highways for carpools. These are groups of three or more people who drive to and from work together. They share the costs of gas and parking and take turns driving into the city.

Getting to work and getting home can be difficult in many different places around the world. Rush hour traffic seems to be a universal problem.

I. TRUE or FALSE? Write T if the sentence is true, and F if it is false.

—— 1. All commuters have cars or bicycles.
—— 2. There are historic sites in Athens and Rome.
—— 3. In Seoul, people have to pay double the normal taxi fare.
—— 4. Rush hour is only a problem in Athens, Rome, Seoul, Washington, D.C., and other cities in the United States.
—— 5. In Washington, D.C., commuters have to drive to work in carpools.

II. DID YOU UNDERSTAND? Circle the letter of the correct answer.

1. Big cities have problems during rush hour because there are
   a. special lanes on highways.
   b. many commuters.
   c. four rush hours.

2. Most of the commuters in Tokyo
   a. take trains to work.
   b. are "packers."
   c. take taxis.

3. It took a long time to build a subway system in Rome because
   a. the streets are very crowded.
   b. the workers discovered many artifacts and places of interest.
   c. there are many historic sites.

4. Commuters in carpools probably
   a. live in the city.
   b. take the subway to work.
   c. save money on gas and parking lot fees.

5. All carpools
   a. are a universal problem.
   b. have more than one person.
   c. have special license plates.

CHECK-UP TEST: Chapters 1, 2, 3

A. Fill in the blanks.

Example ___How___ are you?
Fine.

1. _____ do you want to know?
Your telephone number.

2. _____ are you from?
Barcelona.

3. _____ is your teacher?
Mrs. Frank.

4. _____ are things?
All right.

5. _____ do you do?
I'm an accountant.

6. _____ did you get here?
At 9:30.

7. _____ are you leaving?
I've got to go home and study.

8. _____ car did you use?
Jim's.

9. _____ did you hear that?
In the hallway.

B. Fill in the blanks.

Example They plan to go ___on___ strike.

1. What's your date _____ birth?

2. He lives _____ the third floor.

3. Where _____ New York are you from?

4. I'd like the number _____ Joe Tyler.

5. Let me introduce you _____ Jeff.

6. Which department do you work _____?

7. We don't know _____ sure.

8. She has plans _____ the weekend.

9. Tell me a little _____ yourself.

10. The supermarket is _____ the left.

11. Are you _____ me so far?

C. Complete the conversation.

You're new here, aren't you?
    Yes, I am.

My name is Bill Jolson. ___What's your name___?   1
    I'm Fred Peterson.

_____?   2
    I started working here last Monday.

_____?   3
    I'm working in the Personnel Department.

_____?   4
    I'm enjoying it very much.

I'm glad to hear that. Nice meeting you, Fred.

D. Which sentence means the same? Put a ✔ next to the best answer.

Example   Pardon me.
    _____ Tell me.
    ✔ Excuse me.
    _____ Not much.

1. Nice meeting you.
    _____ I'd like to meet you.
    _____ I'm glad to meet you.
    _____ Let me introduce you.

2. What's your date of birth?
    _____ Is today your birthday?
    _____ When is your birthday?
    _____ What's the date?

3. How are things?
    _____ What do you do?
    _____ Who are you?
    _____ How are you doing?

4. I don't know for sure.
    _____ Sure.
    _____ I'm not positive.
    _____ I'm sure.

5. What do you do?
    _____ How are you?
    _____ What about you?
    _____ What's your occupation?

6. What's wrong?
    _____ What's the matter?
    _____ What a shame!
    _____ What's new?

7. She's pretty sure she'll come.
    _____ She's really beautiful.
    _____ She'll probably come.
    _____ I'm certain she'll come.

8. I'd like you to meet Jim.
    _____ I'm glad to meet Jim.
    _____ Tell me a little about Jim.
    _____ I'd like to introduce you to Jim.

9. I'm very sorry to hear that.
    _____ I apologize.
    _____ That's too bad!
    _____ I don't know for sure.

E. Circle the word that doesn't belong.

Example   teacher   driver   (gym)   accountant

1. monorail   city   plane   bus
2. street   interstate   exit   avenue
3. think   certain   positive sure
4. okay   all right   fine   now
5. flight   platform   pier   gate

F. Listen and circle the best response.

Example
    a. Yes, I was.
    (b.) I'm from Rome.
    c. Last year.

1. a. I'm not.
   b. Yes, I am.
   c. Not much.

2. a. Yes.
   b. I've got to go.
   c. I have to get it.

3. a. I watched TV.
   b. I'll probably stay home.
   c. I'm a journalist.

4. a. I know.
   b. I suppose so.
   c. You, too.

5. a. About a year.
   b. Personnel.
   c. Very much.

6. a. The last part.
   b. Sure.
   c. That's right.

7. a. Gate 11.
   b. At noon.
   c. Yes, it is.

8. a. I need some information.
   b. Can you spell that?
   c. On the elevator.

4

A. WHAT KIND IS IT?
Student Course Book pp. 30–31

Circle the correct answer.

1. It's a [quiet / **brand new**] stove.
2. This is a [friendly / convenient] dog.
3. These cabinets are very [friendly / clean].
4. The rent is [reasonable / safe].
5. Is it a [desirable / comfortable] neighborhood?
6. The neighbors are [quiet / like].
7. The building is [allowed / safe].
8. Elevators are [convenient / correct].

B. A TWO-BEDROOM APARTMENT?
Student Course Book pp. 30–31

Complete the conversation. Fill in the missing lines with an appropriate question.

1. I'm looking for an apartment with two bedrooms.
   A two-bedroom apartment? Let me check.
2. We can take a break for twenty minutes.
   _____? Let's get a cup of coffee!
3. This will be a meal with four courses!
   _____? Fantastic!
4. My fiancé just gave me a diamond. It has forty carats!
   _____? Let me see!
5. Do you know a gas station that is open twenty-four hours?
   _____? Yes. Take the next left.
6. We need a garage for two cars.
   _____? Hmm. Let me see.

C. MATCHING

Student Course Book pp. 30–31

apt. = apartment	kit. = kitchen
a/c = air conditioning	lge. = large
avail. = available	loc. = location
BR = bedroom	mo. = month
bldg. = building	mod. = modern
conv. = convenient	trans. = transportation
elec. = electricity	utils. = utilities
fpl. = fireplace	W/D = washer & dryer
incl. = including	w/ = with

_c_ 1. 2 BR
___ 2. 2 apts. avail.
___ 3. 1 BR apt.
___ 4. w/ mod. kit.
___ 5. incl. utils.
___ 6. lge. BR
___ 7. near trans.
___ 8. conv. loc.
___ 9. $400 mo.
___ 10. w/fpl.
___ 11. w/a/c
___ 12. w/W/D

a. with a modern kitchen
b. air conditioning
c. a two-bedroom apartment
d. near transportation
e. including utilities
f. two apartments
g. a washer and dryer
h. a large bedroom
i. four hundred a month
j. a one-bedroom apartment
k. fireplace
l. convenient location

D. CLASSIFIED ADS

Student Course Book pp. 30–31

These people are looking for apartments. Which apartment would they want to see?

A. DOWNTOWN AREA/123 Kent St.
2BR, a/c, fpl, conv. loc.
$650 mo. plus utils.
276-1274

B. PARK HILL/160 Park Rd.
2 lge. 1 BR apts. avail.,
mod. kit. $595 + utils.
622-0567

C. 143 Spring Rd. 3BR
W/D, fpl, conv. trans. $750
mo. + utils. 524-3920

D. OAK VALLEY/4356 Oak Ave.
2BR lge. kit. a/c, $550
mo. incl. utils. 338-5608

1. "We're looking for a three-bedroom apartment." 1. _C_
2. "I'd like an apartment with air conditioning and a fireplace." 2. ___
3. "We need a washer and dryer in the apartment." 3. ___
4. "We'd like a two-bedroom, but we can't pay more than $600." 4. ___
5. "I need a one-bedroom apartment." 5. ___
6. "Do you have an apartment downtown?" 6. ___
7. "I'd like an apartment with a modern kitchen." 7. ___
8. "Is there anything available in Oak Valley?" 8. ___
9. "We're going to need two apartments." 9. ___
10. "We'd like the utilities included in our rent." 10. ___

E. WE'RE OUT OF ...

Student Course Book pp. 32–33

Circle the correct words.

1. We need [(a few) / a little] apples, [a few / a little] lemons, and [a / some] yogurt.

   Okay. Do you want me to get [a / some] milk, too?

2. How [many / much] sugar do you want me to get?

   A large bag. I guess we also need [a little / a few] margarine.

3. Can I get [a / some] loaf of whole wheat bread?

   Sure. And how about [a / some] cheese and [a few / a little] wine?

4. Do you need [a / some] money from the bank?

   No, thanks. I have [a few / a little] dollars.

F. MATCHING

Student Course Book pp. 32–33

Draw a line to the correct words for each group.

1. What else —————————— anything else?
2. Could you do me   a big favor?
3. Can you tell us —————————— can you tell us?

4. Let's   very much.
5. Let   me see.
6. Thanks   check.

7. We're   of cash.
8. We'd   like a reasonable rent.
9. We're out   looking for a new apartment.

G. SHOPPING LISTS

Student Course Book pp. 32–33

can	bag	gallon	box
tube	liter	pound	

1. The Milfords are going to have a party tonight. Complete their shopping list.

Don't forget....	
a can of	tuna fish
	potato chips
	crackers
	cheese

bunch	six-pack	loaf	stick
dozen	pint	jar	head

2. A few of Nancy's friends are going to visit her tomorrow afternoon. Complete Nancy's shopping list.

Don't forget....	
	bread
	grapes
	soda
	mayonnaise
	butter

tube	jar	box	container
loaf	head	gallon	

3. Mrs. King's grandchildren are planning to visit her for the weekend. Complete her shopping list.

Don't forget....	
	milk
	peanut butter
	white bread
	toothpaste
	cookies

gallon	container	bottle	bag
stick	dozen	can	liter

4. It's Tommy's birthday. His mother is going to make his favorite cake. Complete her shopping list.

Don't forget....	
	eggs
	sugar
	vanilla ice cream
	margarine
	yogurt

 H. LISTENING

Student Course Book pp. 32–33

Listen and complete the sentence.

1. 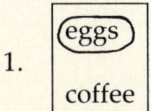 (eggs) / coffee

2. tuna / ice cream

3. white wine / peanut butter

4. lemons / toothpaste

5. ground beef / rice

6. lettuce / cheese

7. butter / onion

8. tomatoes / sugar

I. MATCH AND PRACTICE   Student Course Book p. 34

Draw a line to the correct response for each group.

1. Where's the milk?   Imported Foods.
2. Where can I find taco shells?   Household Supplies.
3. Can you tell me where the sponges are?   Dairy Section.

4. I need to find avocados.   Frozen Foods.
5. Where are the napkins?   Produce.
6. Can you tell me where I can find TV dinners?   Paper Products.

Now practice conversations based on the exercises.

Example   Pardon me.   Where's the milk?
             The milk?   It's in the Dairy Section, Aisle 11.
             Thank you.

J. EXCUSE ME . . .   Student Course Book p. 34

Circle the correct word.

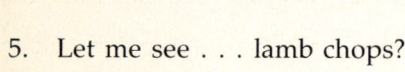

1. Sugar?   Let me see. [(It's) / They're] in Aisle 12.

2. Hmm.   Toothpicks? [It's / They're] in the Produce Department.

3. Jack, could you get the apple cider? [It's / They're] in Aisle 14.

4. Hair spray? [It's / They're] in Aisle 2.

5. Let me see . . . lamb chops? [It's / They're] in Frozen Foods.

6. Could you please pick up the dog food, Mary? [It's / They're] in the next aisle.

7. Are you looking for spaghetti? [It's / They're] in the last aisle.

34

K. LISTENING

Student Course Book p. 34

Listen to the sentence. Circle the correct answer.

1. ③ / C
2. 8 / H
3. A / J
4. 8 / A
5. C / D
6. G / J
7. 4 / 14
8. M / N
9. 70 / 17
10. S / F

L. THAT'LL BE $20.81

Student Course Book p. 35

1. How much was the wine? __$5.99__
2. What cost ninety cents? _____
3. How much was the garlic? _____
4. What kind of yogurt did he buy? _____
5. Did the customer buy a quart or a pint of skim milk? _____
6. How much was the tax? _____
7. What was the date? _____
8. How much did the customer give the cashier? _____
9. How much change did the cashier give the customer? _____

```
skim mlk qt         .99
margarine          1.14
2 onions            .90
orange yogurt       .68
bread              1.35
red wine           5.99
spaghetti           .89
garlic              .79
ice cream pt        .65
TAX                 .87

TOTAL             14.25
CASH              20.00
CHANGE DUE         5.75
02/06/88    17:45 PM
THANK YOU, COME AGAIN
```

M. CHECK THE PRICES!

Student Course Book p. 35

SWISS CHEESE
You pay: Unit Price:
1.29   4.13 per pound

STAR CEREAL
You pay: Unit Price:
1.72   2.75 per pound

1/2 gal. skim milk
You pay: Unit Price:
1.13   2.26 gal.

1. How much does the customer have to pay for the box of cereal? _____
2. How much is the cheese per pound? _____

GROUND BEEF   sell by FEB 22
1.69 price $1.66
per pound   TOTAL PRICE

3. How much does the customer have to pay for the package of ground beef? _____
4. Does the package contain a pound of beef? _____
5. How much is a half-gallon of skim milk? _____

N. LISTENING

Student Course Book p. 35

Listen to each sentence.   Circle the correct price.

1. $14.50 / **($13.15)**
2. $ 8.10 / $18.10
3. $11.40 / $ 7.40
4. $16.43 / $ 6.43
5. $15.76 / $14.66
6. $30.58 / $13.58
7. $22.11 / $22.87
8. $18.98 / $19.88

O. WHAT'S IN IT?

Student Course Book p. 36

| it | It's |
| them | They're |

| a few | a little |

1. Mmm! This apple pie is delicious! What's in ___it___?

   _____ apples, of course, _____ sugar, _____ flour, _____ raisins, _____ butter, and _____ lemon juice.

   _____ fantastic!

2. These rolls are wonderful! What do you put in _____?

   I use _____ margarine, _____ whole wheat flour, _____ eggs, _____ milk, _____ raisins, and _____ cinnamon.

   _____ great!

P. LISTENING

Student Course Book p. 36

Listen to each sentence.   Circle the correct word.

1. **(egg rolls)** / utilities
2. flour / cabbage
3. pork / mall
4. house / refrigerator
5. homework / lemon
6. apartment / dog

Q. FOLLOW THE RECIPE   Student Course Book p. 37

Draw a line to the correct words for each group.

1. Do I bake them at   the kitchen?
2. Could I ask for   the recipe?
3. Did you clean   450 degrees?

4. You'll need to put in two   hot water.
5. Add half a pound of   beef.
6. Put in three teaspoons of   eggs.

7. Put it into a greased   an hour.
8. Bake for   milk.
9. Add a cup of   pan.

10. I've   it.
11. It's really   got it.
12. I like   very easy.

R. MY FAVORITE RECIPE   Student Course Book p. 37

Write your favorite recipe.

You'll really like this!   It's very easy to make.   First, ...

S. READING: *Food Markets* Student Course Book p. 37

In some parts of the United States, there are enormous supermarkets with aisles and aisles of different kinds of foods and products. For example, you can find fifteen to twenty different kinds of cheese in the Dairy section. You can find many different brands of toilet tissue in the Paper Products section. The Frozen Food section has everything from cans of frozen apple juice to bags of mixed vegetables, from ice cream to frozen pizza.

Many supermarkets also have a big Health Care Products aisle. This section is like a small drug store. It has different brands of medicines, shampoos, toothpastes, and other health care items. Some supermarkets even sell magazines, books, shoes, underwear, hammers, screwdrivers, and other household products.

The supermarkets offer services, too. You can leave your film there and return the next day to get your photographs. You can use a special card in the "money machines" and take money out of your bank. In some supermarkets, you can rent floor polishers, carpet cleaners, and even movies!

Shoppers in many supermarkets can buy snacks and cold drinks from vending machines. In some places, tired, hungry shoppers can even sit down and enjoy a fresh cup of coffee and a doughnut at a supermarket snack bar or coffee shop.

These huge supermarkets with their large variety of goods and services are not the only kind of food markets in the United States. There are smaller grocery stores in many cities. These stores usually carry the same food products as the large supermarkets, but they don't usually have as wide a selection. Grocery stores are often in locations convenient for people who don't drive. Some cities also have specialty stores such as fish markets, butcher shops, and bakeries. Years ago, these little shops were very common, but in many places, they are less common today. Supermarkets, with their variety of products and services, are much more popular.

I. TRUE or FALSE?   Put a T if the sentence is true, and F if the sentence is false.

_____ 1. People can find different kinds of food markets in the United States.

_____ 2. People have to go to supermarkets to buy household products.

_____ 3. Most shoppers in the United States go to specialty stores.

_____ 4. Neighborhood grocery stores are usually enormous.

_____ 5. Shoppers can eat and drink at some supermarkets.

II. DID YOU UNDERSTAND?   Circle the letter of the correct answer.

1. The Health Care Products aisle in a supermarket has
   a. items you can find in drug stores.
   b. medicines only.
   c. everything you can find in drug stores.

2. At many supermarkets, you can
   a. watch movies.
   b. take money out of your bank account.
   c. find smaller grocery stores.

3. At a butcher shop, you can probably buy
   a. butchers.
   b. special pizza.
   c. different kinds of meat.

4. Neighborhood grocery stores carry many items, but
   a. not many different types.
   b. aren't in convenient locations.
   c. are only for people who don't have cars.

5. Supermarkets are becoming
   a. specialty shops.
   b. more and more expensive.
   c. more common than grocery stores.

5

A. HAVE YOU . . . ? Student Course Book p. 40

Have you driven a truck before?	Has she driven a truck before?	drive	drove	driven
Yes, I have.	Yes, she has.	take	took	taken
No, I haven't.	No, she hasn't.	do	did	done
		write	wrote	written
		use	used	used
		work	worked	worked
		talk	talked	talked

1. Have you ___written___ the letter to the Acme Corporation?

    No, _____.

2. Has he ever _____ as a cashier before?

    Yes, _____.

3. Have Jane and Billy _____ their homework?

    No, _____.

4. Has she _____ a car with a manual transmission before?

    Yes, _____.

5. Has Ms. Kelly _____ inventory before?

    No, _____.

6. Has your parrot ever _____?

    Yes, _____.

7. Have the secretaries _____ the new word processor yet?

    Yes, _____.

B. WROTE OR WRITTEN? Student Course Book p. 40

1. I haven't [**written** / wrote] to my brother in several months.

2. My cousin [taken / **took**] me to the circus last weekend.

3. Tommy hasn't [drove / driven] a car before.

4. Has the new mechanic [did / done] a good job this week?

5. The manager [written / wrote] a long report about the problem.

6. Have you [took / taken] your medicine yet?

C. WE NEED A GOOD . . .

Student Course Book p. 40

| dishwasher | bookkeeper | delivery person | stock clerk |
| reporter | cashier | mechanic's assistant | |

1. We need a good _____reporter_____ who can write about sports.

2. I haven't worked as a _____ before, but I'm sure I could learn how to drive a car with a manual transmission.

3. We're looking for an experienced _____. We need someone who has taken inventory before.

4. We need an experienced _____. Have you done tune-ups before?

5. I've operated kitchen equipment before. Could I apply for the job as a _____?

6. I've never worked as a _____ before, but I'm sure I could learn to use a computerized cash register.

7. We're going to need a _____ soon. Have you written paychecks before?

D. WHICH WORD?

Student Course Book p. 41

| May   Can |

1. _____Can_____ you type?

| Do   May |

2. _____ I request an interview?

| Can   Do |

3. _____ you have experience?

| Is   May |

4. _____ tomorrow convenient for you?

| Could   May |

5. _____ you come in to fill out an application form?

| May   Do |

6. _____ you have a college degree?

| Can   May |

7. _____ you work weekends?

| May   Am |

8. _____ I have an application form?

E. WHICH QUESTION?

Choose the correct question.

1. a. That position it is still open?
   b. That position is it still open?
   (c.) Is that position still open?

2. a. An interview may I request?
   b. May I request an interview?
   c. I may request an interview?

3. a. With you it is all right?
   b. It is with you all right?
   c. Is it all right with you?

4. a. You have previous experience?
   b. Do you have previous experience?
   c. Previous experience, do you have?

5. a. Is it convenient for you?
   b. It is for you convenient?
   c. It is convenient for you?

6. a. Have you training professional?
   b. Do you have professional training?
   c. You have professional training?

F. MATCHING

benes. = benefits	immed. = immediately
bkgrd. = background	nec. = necessary
driv. lic. = driver's license	pers. = person
eves. = evenings	pref. = preferred
excel. = excellent	P/T = part-time
exp. = experience	F/T = full-time
gd. = good	req. = required
/hr. = per hour	sal. = salary
	sec. = secretarial

_f_ 1. $5 per hour
____ 2. exp. nec.
____ 3. P/T eves.
____ 4. driv. lic. req.
____ 5. gd. sal.
____ 6. excel. benes.
____ 7. apply in pers.
____ 8. F/T only
____ 9. start immed.
____ 10. sec. bkgrd. pref.

a. must have experience
b. good salary
c. driver's license required
d. secretarial background preferred
e. start immediately
f. five dollars an hour
g. full-time position only
h. excellent benefits
i. part-time evenings
j. apply in person

G. CLASSIFIED ADS

These people are looking for jobs. Which job would they want to apply for?

A. DRIVERS-P/T only. driv. lic. req. $4/hr. start immed. Pizza People 589-2111

B. MEDICAL ASST/SEC. med. exp. req. F/T, exc. sal. Call 982-2421

C. RESTAURANT-Claude's Place-gd trng. gd pay excel. benes. PT eves. Apply in pers.

_B_ 1. "I need a full-time job."

____ 2. "I'm looking for a job in a restaurant."

____ 3. "I'd like to get a part-time job as a driver."

____ 4. "I was a secretary for Dr. Jones for four years."

____ 5. "I don't know how to drive, but I need a part-time job."

____ 6. "I need a part-time job with benefits."

H. WHICH WORD IS RIGHT?

1. He has managed a large housekeeping [license / (staff)].

2. Louis was a medical [experience / assistant] for three years.

3. Is the position of [computerized / administrative] assistant still open?

4. I haven't driven a car with a [trilingual / manual] transmission before.

5. A college [university / degree] is required.

6. We're looking for someone with a [background / transmission] in medical administration.

I. HAVE YOU EVER...?

1. Have you ever made popcorn in a microwave oven?

    No, __I haven't__, but __I've made__ almost everything else in a microwave!

    | I / We / You / They | haven't. | I've / We've / You've / They've | done that before. |
    | He / She / It | hasn't. | He's / She's / It's | |

2. Has Ursula ever ridden a motorcycle?

    No, _____, but _____ a moped.

3. Have the Bensons ever flown to California?

    No, _____, but _____ to Europe many times.

4. Has George ever given piano lessons?

    No, _____, but _____ guitar lessons.

5. Have you ever sung in front of people?

    No, _____, but _____ a lot in the shower!

J. THE BABY-SITTER

Student Course Book p. 42

Joey's parents are at the movies tonight. He's giving the baby-sitter a lot of trouble. Complete the sentences and practice the conversation with another student.

Joey, please put away your toys.

    *I've already put away*₁ my toys!

Okay. Do you want to sing a song?

    No. _____₂ a song today.

Hmm. Do you want to take a bath?

    No. _____₃ a bath today.

Well, would you like to ride your bicycle in the basement?

    No. _____₄ it today.

Well, what do you want to do?

    I don't know. _____₅ everything.

Then go to bed!

    Aw, gee!

K. HOW LONG? SINCE WHEN?

Student Course Book p. 43

1. Do you know how to type?

    Yes. *I've been typing* for a long time.

2. Is Kathy taking inventory now?

    Yes. _____ inventory since this morning.

I've / We've / You've / They've } been living here since 1985.
He's / She's / It's }

3. Do they do tune-ups at the gas station?

    Yes. _____ tune-ups there since 1983.

4. Can Fred sell office furniture?

    Yes. _____ office furniture for two years.

5. Is it snowing?

    Yes. _____ since midnight.

6. Can you use a word processor?

    Yes. _____ word processors for a long time.

L. SINCE OR FOR?

Student Course Book p. 43

since	for
since 1980	**for** a long time
since last week	**for** two weeks
since yesterday afternoon	**for** the past year
since I was a teenager	**for** many days

1. I've been studying at this school __since__ last year.
2. Miss Walters has been working here _____ five years.
3. They've been living in New York _____ their college days.
4. It's been snowing in the mountains _____ two days.
5. Joey has been doing his homework _____ he came home.
6. We've been waiting at this bus stop _____ an hour.
7. He's been selling stereo equipment _____ last year.

M. WHAT'S YOUR ANSWER?

Student Course Book p. 44

Circle the best response.

1. Did you work as a secretary?
   a. Yes, I did.
   b. Yes, I have.

2. Has she found a job?
   a. No, she hasn't.
   b. No, she didn't.

3. Are you taking lessons now?
   a. Yes. I took them for five years.
   b. Yes. I've been taking them for five years.

4. Are you working in the cafeteria?
   a. Yes. I've been working there for a year.
   b. Yes. I worked there for a year.

5. How long have you lived here?
   a. I lived here for two months.
   b. I've been living here for a year.

6. Did you study there for a long time?
   a. Yes. I've been studying there for three years.
   b. Yes. I was there for three years.

N. A JOB INTERVIEW

Student Course Book p. 44

How long have you __been__₁ working at Globe Motors?

_____₂ last year.

Where _____₃ you work before that?

I _____₄ at Systems Mechanics _____₅ three years.

_____₆ you _____₇ as a mechanic _____₈ a long time?

Yes. _____₉ _____₁₀ _____₁₁ as a mechanic _____₁₂ 1975.

O. LISTENING

Student Course Book p. 44

Listen and circle the correct sentence.

1. a. He takes lessons now.
   (b.) He isn't taking lessons now.

2. a. She's a student.
   b. She doesn't study English now.

3. a. He's an architect.
   b. He worked as an architect.

4. a. She's in college.
   b. She's a computer analyst.

5. a. I work in Accounting.
   b. I worked in Accounting.

6. a. We live in that building.
   b. We've moved.

7. a. She's a receptionist.
   b. She's been a receptionist.

8. a. They're planning the meeting.
   b. They planned the meeting.

P. JOB RESPONSIBILITIES: NOW AND BEFORE

Student Course Book p. 45

Circle the correct words.

1. In my present job, (I've been planning) / I planned international meetings.

2. I've done / I did the payroll in my last position.

3. I'm / I've been a bookkeeper for a long time.

4. In my current job, I've been supervising / I supervised new employees.

5. I haven't done / didn't do performance evaluations since last year.

6. I've ordered / I ordered all the office supplies in the job I had before.

7. I've performed / I performed many different blood tests in my current position.

8. In my last job, I was / I've been in charge of the benefits program.

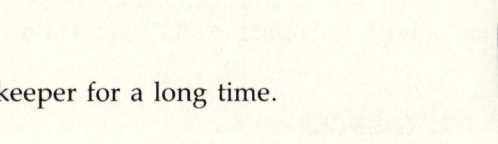

Q. NICK'S RESUME Student Course Book p. 45

RESUME

Nick Maxwell
4562 Tyler St., Apt. 3C
Los Angeles, CA 90021
(213) 345-6982

JOB OBJECTIVE

I would like to find a position as an Auto Service Supervisor.

EDUCATION

City Community College, Los Angeles, California, currently majoring in Industrial Education.

Jackson High School, Los Angeles, California. I graduated in June 1984. I finished a one-year program called Introduction to Auto Mechanics.

WORK EXPERIENCE

AUTO SERVICE MANAGER: Central Rent-a-Car, Los Angeles, California, from June 1984 to present. My primary responsibility is to oversee ten mechanics. I order all supplies and I handle all customer problems.

AUTO MECHANIC: Jack's Auto Shop, Los Angeles, California, from May 1982 to May 1984. I worked on many different kinds of cars, especially European and Japanese models.

REFERENCES

Charles Wright, instructor of Industrial Education, City Community College, Los Angeles, CA, 445-9865.

Jack Robinson, Jack's Auto Shop, 234 Los Alamos Drive, Los Angeles, CA, 342-7678.

---

1. Where is Nick working now?

   He's working at Central Rent-a-Car.

2. How long has he been working there?

3. Where did he work before that?

4. How long did he work there?

5. What has Nick been studying at college?

6. What kind of job is he looking for?

R. YOUR RESUME Student Course Book p. 45

(Name) _____

(Address) _____

_____

(Telephone Number) _____

JOB OBJECTIVE

_____

_____

EDUCATION

_____

_____

_____

_____

_____

WORK EXPERIENCE

_____

_____

_____

_____

_____

_____

_____

REFERENCES

_____

_____

_____

_____

_____

S. SOME QUESTIONS AT THE INTERVIEW

Student Course Book p. 46

Complete the questions and answers.

1. How long __have you been__ married?
   __I've been married__ for five years.

2. _____ have any children?
   Yes. _____ a boy and a girl.

3. _____ living here a long time?
   Yes. _____ since 1978.

4. _____ ever supervised a large staff?
   No. But _____ a staff of three people.

5. Do you think you'd _____ train new employees?
   Yes. _____ training new employees for a long time.

6. Why _____ leave your last position?
   _____ because I wanted to work for a larger company.

7. _____ any other questions?
   No. _____ answered all my questions already.

T. AT THE JOB

Student Course Book p. 46

Draw a line to the correct words for each group.

1. You need to give your boss two weeks ——— vacation.
2. You can take 45 minutes for your   notice.
3. You've earned fifteen days of   lunch break.

4. What else would you like to   questions?
5. Do you have any further   available?
6. When would you be   know?

7. I need to talk to my present   positive.
8. I learned quickly at my current   employer.
9. I'm absolutely   job.

U. **READING:** *The Job Interview* Student Course Book p. 46

When a job opening is advertised in the United States, there are often a lot of people interested in applying. Many job hunters send in their resumes and apply for the same position. Sometimes a company will receive hundreds of resumes for a single job opening. The job interview, therefore, is very important. In the interview, an applicant must demonstrate that he or she is the best person for the job.

Because job interviews are so critical, some job hunters read books or take courses to help them make a good first impression. These books and courses are full of advice and suggestions to help job applicants prepare for their interviews. For example, successful applicants dress appropriately and have a clean and neat appearance. They take their resume or a sheet of paper listing their education and work experience with them to the interview. They also prepare a list of questions about the job or the company. They go to the interview alone and are always on time.

At the beginning of the interview, the applicant shakes hands firmly with the employer. The employer usually invites the applicant to sit down. During the interview, it is appropriate to smile often and to look directly into the eyes of the interviewer. The applicant doesn't chew gum or smoke during the interview. The applicant is prepared to answer questions about education and previous jobs. More difficult questions are possible, such as: "Why did you leave your last position?" Sometimes interviewers also try to get to know the applicant better. They ask questions about the applicant's personal background, family, and hobbies. Interviewers expect applicants to talk proudly, confidently, and truthfully about their work experience, skills, goals, and abilities. When the interview is over, the applicant stands up, shakes hands with the interviewer, and says thank you for the time the person has offered.

Job applicants who can show they are capable, well-prepared, punctual, polite, and honest have a better chance of getting the job they're looking for.

I. TRUE or FALSE?   Write T if the sentence is true, and F if it is false.

____ 1. Job hunters often have interviews with employers before they apply.

____ 2. It's important to perform well during job interviews.

____ 3. Job applicants really shouldn't ask any questions during an interview.

____ 4. Most employers think experience is the most important quality to have.

____ 5. Employers sometimes ask questions about the applicant's family and personal life.

II. DID YOU UNDERSTAND?   Circle the correct answer.

1. The job interview is important because
   a. all the applicants for a single position have to have interviews.
   b. the applicant must show that he or she is capable for the job.
   c. the applicant must be on time.

2. When an applicant smiles during an interview, it is considered
   a. polite and friendly.
   b. funny.
   c. a mistake.

3. Job hunters read books and take courses
   a. after they have successful job interviews.
   b. if they are well-prepared.
   c. to prepare themselves for their job interviews.

4. It's important to be punctual for a job interview because
   a. even women shake hands.
   b. it is considered impolite to be late.
   c. job applicants should always be neat and clean.

5. It's a good idea to talk about all your skills and abilities during the interview, but it's not a good idea to
   a. be independent.
   b. look directly into the eyes of the interviewer.
   c. lie.

6

A. EMERGENCY!
Student Course Book p. 50

| an ambulance | an animal removal specialist | a squad car |
| a repairman | an engine unit | |

1. Our telephone wires have just fallen down.

    We'll send _____a repairman_____ right away.

2. There's a squirrel in our basement!

    We'll send _____ immediately.

3. Someone has just broken into my neighbor's garage!

    We'll send _____ right now.

4. A fire has just broken out in the apartment across the hall.

    We'll send _____ immediately.

5. I think my grandfather has just had a heart attack!

    We'll send _____ right away.

B. LISTENING
Student Course Book p. 50

Listen and circle the correct sentence.

1. a. There's a fire.
   b. Someone hurt his chin.

2. a. They need two men.
   b. Something has to be fixed.

3. a. Someone has just broken in.
   b. His neighbor is a robber.

4. a. She's at the bottom of the steps.
   b. Her flight has just landed.

5. a. They have to go to the zoo right away.
   b. There's a strange noise in the fireplace.

6. a. A repairman needs to fix the dishwasher.
   b. They have to call the Fire Department.

7. a. They need to go to the post office.
   b. There's been a medical emergency.

8. a. They need to call the police.
   b. They'll send a repairman.

9. a. Someone should call the ASPCA.
   b. Someone should call an ambulance.

10. a. Someone needs the police.
    b. Someone needs a mechanic.

50

C. WHERE?

Student Course Book p. 51

1. I saw an accident [across / (in front of)] the school.

2. I lost my homework [near / on] the bus stop.

3. A man has been mugged [in / at] the corner [from / of] Tenth and F Street.

4. The plane finally landed safely [on / from] the runway.

5. The robbery occurred [at / across] the street [from / on] the parking lot.

6. It happened [on / down] the street [of / from] my office.

D. SOMEONE HAS BEEN MUGGED . . .

Student Course Book p. 51

1. Someone has [(been mugged) / mugged] at the bus stop.

2. Their plane has just [landed / was landed].

3. Two houses in our neighborhood [have robbed / have been robbed] this week.

4. Some skaters [have fallen / were fallen] through the ice at the town pond.

5. A young boy has [run over / been run over] by a car!

6. A big truck [has overturned / been overturned] on the expressway.

E. LISTENING

Student Course Book p. 51

Listen to the conversation. Then listen to the sentence and circle *True* or *False*.

1. True   (False)
2. True   False
3. True   False
4. True   False
5. True   False
6. True   False
7. True   False
8. True   False

F. YOU'LL FIND IT

Student Course Book p. 52

1. It's [(next to) / on] the hair spray.
2. You can find it [in / on] Aisle 5.
3. They're [up / on] the top shelf.
4. It's [on / in] the right.
5. Did you find it [in / on] the back of the store?
6. You'll see them [near / next] the eyedrops.
7. It's located [from / in] this section.
8. The spray is [in / on] the next aisle.

G. LISTENING

Student Course Book p. 52

Listen to the sentence. Circle the problem.

1. weather / (dry skin)
2. nose / hair
3. frizzy hair / headache
4. cough / hair
5. watery eyes / rainy day
6. cough / dry hair

H. MEDICAL PROBLEMS

Student Course Book p. 53

1. He hasn't [(been able to) / can] sleep.
2. She [has been / has] feeling nauseous.
3. Our cat [has / has been] refusing to eat.
4. He [isn't / hasn't] been taking his medicine.
5. I'm not [been able to / able to] move my arm.
6. He's [been feeling / had] a bad toothache.

I. MORE MEDICAL PROBLEMS

Student Course Book p. 53

Fill in the blanks. Then practice the conversations with another student.

1. I'm feeling dizzy.

    How long ___have you been feeling dizzy___?

    ___Since___ yesterday evening.

2. Fred's ear is still ringing.

    How long _____?

    _____ about two days.

3. Mildred hasn't been able to move her arm.

    How long _____?

    _____ yesterday afternoon.

4. My daughter has a toothache.

    How long _____?

    _____ she woke up.

5. My two-year-old son has a bad cough.

    How long _____?

    _____ about two days.

J. PERSONAL QUESTIONS

Student Course Book p. 53

1. How long have you been studying English?

   ....

2. How long have you known your best friend?

   ....

3. How long have you lived in your present home?

   ....

4. How long has your English teacher been working as a teacher?

   ....

5. How long have you been using this workbook?

   ....

K. MEDICAL HISTORIES

Student Course Book p. 54

Write the questions.

1. <u>Is your son allergic to any medicines</u>?

   No. My son isn't allergic to any medicines.

2. _____?

   Yes. I've had acupuncture before.

3. _____?

   I smoke about ten cigarettes a day.

4. _____?

   No. I haven't had anesthesia before.

5. _____?

   Yes. You have to go on a special diet.

6. _____?

   No. Your mother doesn't have to have surgery.

L. AT THE DOCTOR'S OFFICE

Student Course Book p. 54

1. I don't have any objections to [anesthesia / back trouble].

2. Have you ever had a reaction to [allergies / penicillin]?

3. Has your grandmother ever been [hospitalized / acupuncture]?

4. We need information for your [disease / medical] history.

5. He's had a bad [objection / reaction] to the medicine.

6. She's been having [allergic / back trouble] for a year.

54

M. PATIENT INFORMATION FORM

Last name _____ First name _____ MI _____

Date of birth _____ Sex _____

PATIENT INFORMATION

Address _____ Home Phone _____

Occupation _____ Place of Employment _____

Work Phone _____ Place of Birth _____

Marital Status (please check one) ____ Single ____ Married ____ Divorced ____ Widowed

If married, Spouse's Name _____ Work Phone _____

A. Check any of the following medical problems you now have or have had before:

- ____ weakness
- ____ tiredness
- ____ fever
- ____ night chills
- ____ poor appetite
- ____ dizziness
- ____ nausea
- ____ chest pain
- ____ constipation
- ____ allergies
- ____ headache
- ____ stomachache
- ____ backache
- ____ earache
- ____ coughing
- ____ spitting blood
- ____ vomiting
- ____ watery eyes
- ____ itchy eyes
- ____ ringing ears
- ____ bleeding gums

B. Have you ever ____ been hospitalized?
 ____ had a bad reaction to drugs?
 ____ had surgery? For what reason? _____
 ____ had acupuncture?
 ____ had high blood pressure?

C. Is there a history of any of the following in your family? If yes, indicate who (father, mother, etc.):

Medical Problem	Yes	No	Family Member
Cancer			
Stroke			
Heart disease			
High blood pressure			
TB			
Suicide			

D. Have you had: ____ mumps?   ____ chicken pox?
 ____ measles?   ____ smallpox?
 ____ rubella?   ____ whooping cough?

Do you: ____ take drugs?
 ____ drink alcohol? How often? _____
 ____ smoke? How much? _____

N. THE DOCTOR'S ADVICE

Student Course Book p. 55

Fill in the blank with an appropriate word.

Mr. Wilkins, I strongly __recommend__(1) that you stop smoking.

Hmm. That _____(2) be easy.

I know it won't, but _____(3) really got to. _____(4) essential.

I understand. _____(5) you have any suggestions?

Sure. You _____(6) to promise your wife _____(7) quit. And I _____(8) that you chew gum more often.

I see. _____(9) try to follow your suggestions!

You really _____(10)!

O. MORE MEDICAL ADVICE

Student Course Book p. 55

Circle the answer that is *closest in meaning.*

1. I strongly recommend that you stop.
   a. You can stop.
   b. You've stopped.
   c. You've really got to stop. *(circled)*

2. It's essential for you to change.
   a. You've had to change.
   b. You might change.
   c. You really need to change.

3. Why don't you cut back?
   a. You could cut back.
   b. You think you should cut back.
   c. You must cut back.

4. You have to.
   a. You've really had to.
   b. It's necessary.
   c. You should.

5. You should lose weight.
   a. You must lose weight.
   b. You've been able to lose weight.
   c. You ought to lose weight.

6. It might be a good idea to start exercising.
   a. You could start exercising.
   b. You must start exercising.
   c. It's essential that you start exercising.

P. WHICH WORD?

Student Course Book p. 55

| habits | swimming | diet | lifestyle | lungs | hobby |

1. You really ought to go on a __diet__.

2. I've seen your X-rays, and your _____ are fine.

3. You need to change your eating _____.

4. It might be a good idea to join a _____ class.

5. My _____ is listening to classical music.

6. Your _____ is so busy! You should slow down a little!

Q. **MATCHING** Student Course Book p. 56

| capsule = cap. | tablet = tab. | teaspoons = tsps. | tablespoon = tbsp. |
| after = aft. | before = bef. | once = 1X | twice = 2X |

1. Take two tablets before you eat.
2. Take one teaspoon twice a day.
3. Take two tablespoons once a day.
4. Take a capsule after you eat.
5. Take two teaspoons three times a day.

2 tsps. 3X/day
1 cap. aft. meals
2 tabs. bef. meals
1 tsp. 2X/day
2 tbsps. 1X/day

(1 is matched to "2 tabs. bef. meals")

R. **LISTENING** Student Course Book p. 56

Listen to the directions. Put the number under the correct bottle.

(Bottle 3 is labeled "1")

S. **YOU'RE SUPPOSED TO . . .** Student Course Book p. 56

Answer these questions using *supposed to*.

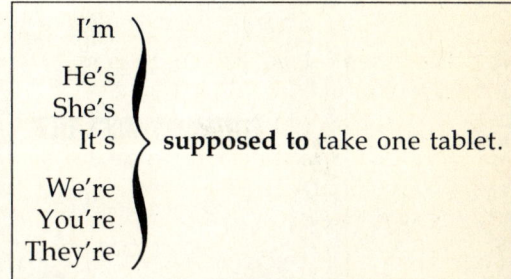

1. What am I supposed to take for a headache?

   __You're supposed to take__ two aspirin.

2. Who are they supposed to call?

   _____ the police.

3. Why is she supposed to have acupuncture?

   _____ acupuncture because she has back trouble.

4. Where is Jack going to meet us?

   _____ us at the library.

5. When does the flight from London land?

   _____ in about half an hour.

6. What time should we get back to the office?

   _____ by 1:30.

7. When should I return his call?

   _____ his call as soon as you can.

T. YOU?   Student Course Book p. 56

| you | you've | you're | your | you'll |

1. __You're__ supposed to take __your__ medicine now.
2. _____ got to follow the directions carefully.
3. It's possible _____ feel sleepy later today.
4. _____ really ought to change _____ lifestyle.
5. _____ got to promise me _____ start exercising.
6. _____ been late every day this week!
7. _____ might get a headache after _____ take these tablets.
8. _____ got to take _____ pills when _____ feeling dizzy.

U. SPEEDY-RELIEF COUGH SYRUP   Student Course Book p. 56

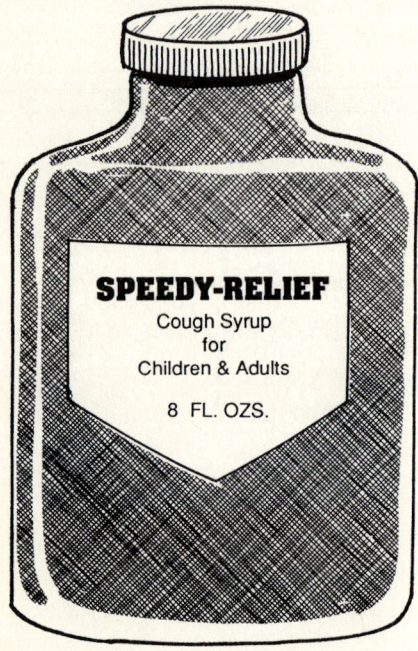

SPEEDY-RELIEF
Cough Syrup
for
Children & Adults
8 FL. OZS.

**DO NOT PURCHASE
IF SEAL IS BROKEN**
Dosage: Adults 2 tsps. every 4 hours.
Children 1/2 tsp. every 4 hours. If
under 2 years of age, consult doctor.
If pregnant, consult your doctor.
If cough continues for more than
1 week, consult your doctor.

EXP July 1992

Circle the correct answer.

1. Speedy-Relief Cough Syrup is for
   a. adults only.
   b. children and adults.
   c. babies.

2. If you are pregnant, you should
   a. take two teaspoons every four hours.
   b. take half a teaspoon every four hours.
   c. talk to your doctor about taking this medicine.

3. Don't buy this syrup
   a. after July 1989.
   b. before you break the seal.
   c. unless you consult your doctor.

4. You should visit the doctor if
   a. you are an adult.
   b. you don't understand the directions on the medicine bottle.
   c. your cough lasts longer than a week.

V. READING: *It Might Work for You*

Student Course Book p. 57

Very often, we have small medical problems that aren't serious enough to require a visit to the doctor's office. Problems such as a sore throat, a stomachache, or a stuffy nose can often be taken care of with "over-the-counter" medicines available on drug store shelves. Many people prefer to treat minor medical problems with "home remedies." These solutions vary from country to country, from family to family, and even from person to person.

For a sore throat, it's certainly easy to stop by a local drug store and pick up a pack of lozenges. But some people prefer to make special drinks, such as warm milk with honey or lemon juice and honey. Others like to gargle with warm salt water.

Stomachaches can be treated with antacids available at local drug stores, but many people first try drinking soda to settle their stomachs. Another, more natural remedy is peppermint tea.

In addition to the various cold medicines available, many people treat their colds by having a bowl of homemade chicken soup or a clove of fresh garlic. Others like to have a "hot toddy," a little whiskey, lemon, honey, and hot water, before they go to bed.

Many books offer helpful suggestions for the treatment of minor medical problems at home and provide useful information about first aid procedures. In the case of a bee sting, for example, they recommend that you put mud or a slice of potato directly on the sting, or a little vinegar on the skin so the sting will disappear.

In the case of a nose bleed, medical guides often suggest three steps to follow in order to help stop the bleeding. First, pinch the nose. Then, tilt the head backward and rest it on the back of a chair. Finally, put an ice pack on the back of the neck. The bleeding should stop within minutes.

For a toothache, take a piece of cotton, pour a little whiskey on it, and put the cotton directly on the aching tooth. This will at least numb the tooth until you can get to a dentist.

Modern medicine has progressed greatly in the past few years, but there are still times when it's very convenient to rely on good old "home remedies."

I. TRUE or FALSE?   Write T if the sentence is true, and F if it is false.

____ 1. It's important to visit the doctor's office very often.

____ 2. It's possible to buy some medicines without going to a doctor.

____ 3. It's essential to drink a "hot toddy" when you have a cold.

____ 4. It's a good idea to look at home medical guides for information about first aid procedures.

____ 5. It's possible to treat a bee sting with a potato.

II. DID YOU UNDERSTAND?   Circle the best answer.

1. Lozenges and antacids are examples of
   a. home remedies.
   b. over-the-counter medicines.
   c. first aid procedures.

2. You can treat a stomachache with
   a. garlic.
   b. an ice pack on the back of the neck.
   c. peppermint tea.

3. Home remedies are convenient to use for
   a. home medical guides.
   b. minor medical problems.
   c. drug store shelves.

4. When you want to treat a sore throat, you should
   a. go to the drug store and buy throat lozenges.
   b. make an appointment to see a doctor.
   c. perform first aid procedures.

5. For nose bleeds or bee stings, you need to know
   a. the names of over-the-counter medicines.
   b. modern medicine.
   c. first aid.

CHECK-UP TEST: *Chapters 4, 5, 6*

A. Circle the correct answer.

Example _____ feeling nauseous.
    a. He
    (b.) He's

1. I know _____ be able to do it.
    a. I'd
    b. I

2. _____ out of coffee.
    a. We'd
    b. We're

3. _____ the matter?
    a. What
    b. What's

4. _____ worried about the test.
    a. I'll
    b. I'm

5. Now _____ got it.
    a. I'll
    b. I've

6. _____ supposed to do it now.
    a. You've
    b. You're

7. _____ suggest this book.
    a. I'm
    b. I'd

8. Do you really like _____?
    a. it
    b. its

9. _____ never been sick.
    a. She
    b. She's

10. Hmm. _____ me see.
    a. Let
    b. Let's

11. _____ might be a good idea.
    a. It's
    b. It

B. Complete the sentence.

Example Can I _____ the manager?
    (a.) speak with
    b. be able to see
    c. like to talk with

1. It's incredible _____!
    a. how much work is there
    b. there is how much work
    c. how much work there is

2. You have _____.
    a. study more often
    b. to study more often
    c. more often to study

3. I've _____ last summer.
    a. been living here since
    b. lived here for
    c. living here since

4. Where _____?
    a. I can find the library
    b. the library can I find
    c. can I find the library

5. I must _____ my homework now.
    a. to do
    b. do
    c. to be doing

6. Do you know _____?
    a. how to type
    b. to type
    c. typing

7. How much _____ me to buy?
    a. you want
    b. do want
    c. do you want

8. Did he _____ his medicine?
    a. took
    b. take
    c. taken

9. _____ be available next week.
    a. I
    b. I'm
    c. I'd

C. Fill in the blank.

| ad | apply | do | experience | for | position | salesperson | would |

Hello. I'm calling about the ____ad____ for a salesclerk.
                                   1

Yes. That _____ is still open. Would you like to _____?
            2   3

Yes, I _____.
         4

Do you have any _____ in sales?
                   5

Yes, I _____. I've been a _____ in a department store
         6   7

_____ three years.
    8

D. Circle the word that doesn't belong.

Example   positive   (absolutely)   certain   sure

1. position   occupation   pleasure   job

2. advise   necessary   urge   recommend

3. popular   wonderful   superb   excellent

4. amazing   unbelievable incredible anything

5. eyedrops   decongestant stuffy   lotion

E. Listen and circle the correct response.

Example a. No, not at the moment.
          (b.) Yes, I have.
           c. Yes, I have four.

1. a. Tuesday is fine.
   b. Two o'clock? That's fine.
   c. Yes, just a few.

2. a. I've finished my chores.
   b. Yes, it's my hat.
   c. Positive.

3. a. I'm an accountant.
   b. I was a driver.
   c. I'd be able to learn.

4. a. For the past five years.
   b. We'll be leaving soon.
   c. About two blocks down the road.

5. a. Yes. It fits perfectly.
   b. Yes. It's very complete.
   c. Yes. Take it to the post office.

6. a. Yes. You've got all of them.
   b. No. What's the last step?
   c. I forgot.

7. a. Sure. What do you want to know?
   b. Certainly. Have a little more.
   c. Yes. Please have another piece.

8. a. Yes. Would you like chocolate?
   b. I've never done it before.
   c. All right. What is it?

9. a. Yes. I think so.
   b. I think ours are noisy.
   c. Yes. They're too loud.

61

7

A. THINGS AND PLACES Student Course Book p. 62

1. You can find beds in the ___Furniture___ Department on the ___first___ floor.

2. Microwave ovens are in the _____ _____ Department on the _____ floor.

3. You'll find stereos in the _____ _____ Department. Take the escalator to the _____ floor.

4. Pots and pans are in the _____ Department in the _____.

5. Girls' dresses? They're in the _____ _____ Department on the _____ floor.

6. I've got to get a dress to wear to my friend's wedding. The _____ _____ Department is on the _____ floor.

7. A tie for your father? Try the _____ _____ Department on the _____ floor.

STORE DIRECTORY	
Children's Clothing	2
Furniture	1
Home Entertainment	3
Household Appliances	1
Housewares	B
Men's Clothing	2
Women's Clothing	2

B. WHERE ARE THESE THINGS LOCATED? Student Course Book p. 62

1. I parked the car near
   a. to the store.
   (b.) the entrance.
   c. the right.

2. Take the elevator to
   a. the third floor.
   b. up.
   c. down one floor.

3. They're on
   a. the rear of the entrance.
   b. the fourth floor.
   c. the basement.

4. We left it at the front of
   a. the building.
   b. the rear.
   c. the flight of stairs.

5. Did they put the boxes in
   a. the side?
   b. the escalator?
   c. the basement?

6. The staircase is on
   a. the left.
   b. the side entrance.
   c. the rear of the store.

C. APPLIANCES AND OTHER THINGS

Student Course Book p. 63

Complete the sentence.

| coffeemaker | computer | gas range | refrigerator | TV | watch |

1. I want to buy the __refrigerator__ with an automatic ice maker.
2. I'd like to look at the _____ that makes twenty cups.
3. We're interested in a _____ with remote control.
4. Do you have a personal _____ at home?
5. He'd like a waterproof _____.
6. My wife and I would like a _____ with a self-cleaning oven.

D. LISTENING

Student Course Book p. 63

Listen to the conversation. Which one are they talking about?

1. (TV) / window
2. watch / coffeemaker
3. computer / refrigerator
4. car / gas range
5. color TV / job
6. clock / computer
7. VCR / ice maker
8. oven / washing machine

(Answer circled for 1: TV)

E. I'M LOOKING FOR . . .

Student Course Book p. 64

Circle the best answer.

1. I'm looking for a
   a. blue light skirt.
   b. light blue skirt. *(circled)*
   c. skirt light blue.

2. She needs a pair of
   a. size 1 sneakers pink.
   b. pink sneakers size 1.
   c. size 1 pink sneakers.

3. He bought a
   a. white shirt permanent press.
   b. white permanent press shirt.
   c. shirt white permanent press.

4. I'll take this
   a. large sweater dark brown.
   b. dark brown large sweater.
   c. large dark brown sweater.

5. I have to find a
   a. long-sleeved size 16 shirt.
   b. shirt long-sleeved size 16.
   c. size 16 long-sleeved shirt.

6. I'd like the
   a. color General Electric small TV.
   b. small color TV General Electric.
   c. small General Electric color TV.

7. I'd like to get the
   a. size 8 light beige coat.
   b. size 8 beige light coat.
   c. light beige size 8 coat.

8. I'm trying to find a
   a. necktie red bright.
   b. red bright necktie.
   c. bright red necktie.

F. AT THE DEPARTMENT STORE

Student Course Book p. 64

Which item would the customer be interested in? Write the letter.

```
a: 15 /33        b: 16 1/2 - 34      c: 15 1/2 - 33         d: 15 - 32
   100% Cotton      100% Polyester      60% Cotton             100% Cotton
                                        40% Polyester
```

__d__ 1. "I wear a size 15 neck and my sleeve length is 32."

_____ 2. "I'd like to find a cotton shirt. My size is 15-33."

_____ 3. "I need a polyester shirt. Size 16½."

_____ 4. "Do you have anything in a cotton/polyester blend?"

```
a: "Kid Town"    b: Women's World    c: "Kid Town"    d: Men's Clothing
   Girls 5          Size 9/10           Boys 8           Style 045/Med
```

_____ 5. "My daughter needs a little dress for her first day of school."

_____ 6. "My husband wears a medium."

_____ 7. "I want to get my sister a nice skirt she can wear to the office."

_____ 8. "I wear a size 8."

```
a: Size 32           b: L   1416         c: Size XL           d: Size 5
   5     1541           Dept.  PRICE        32                   Dept 011
   Dept  Style          11     $11.99       Dept. 245            $16.00
   Price $12.99                             $15.89
```

_____ 9. "This size is too small for me. I think I need a large."

_____ 10. "Size 32, if you have it."

_____ 11. "I'd like to see this in an extra large."

_____ 12. "Do you have these jeans in a size 5?"

G. LISTENING

Student Course Book p. 64

Listen to the conversation.   Circle the words you hear.

1. (size 34) / size 44

2. 15 – 33 / 16 – 33

3. shirt / medium

4. small / 11

5. charge / large

6. pink / Size 12

7. Size 32 / black

8. dress / shirt

H. CAN YOU REMEMBER ALL THOSE SIZES?

Student Course Book p. 64

Some people write their clothing sizes on a small card that they carry in their wallet or purse.

Fill in your sizes:

Clothing	Size
Shirt/Blouse	
Slacks/Pants	
Shoes	
Socks/Stockings	
Belt	
Jacket	

Fill in the sizes of a family member or a friend:

Clothing	Size
Shirt/Blouse	
Slacks/Pants	
Shoes	
Socks/Stockings	
Belt	
Jacket	

I. EXCHANGES

Student Course Book p. 65

Circle the best answer.

1. These sneakers are too tight. I'd like to try _____.
   a. a smaller pair
   b. a more conservative pair
   (c.) a bigger pair

2. Could I exchange this for something more difficult? This is too _____.
   a. weak
   b. simpler
   c. easy

3. This suitcase is a little too heavy. I'd like one that is _____.
   a. more lightweight
   b. more powerful
   c. more difficult

4. My hair is too long. I'd really like it _____.
   a. smaller
   b. shorter
   c. longer

5. This radio is too weak. We need to buy a _____ one.
   a. simpler
   b. fancier
   c. more powerful

6. My husband will think this suit is too fancy. I'd better look at a _____ one.
   a. more conservative
   b. heavier
   c. more lightweight

65

J. LISTENING

Student Course Book p. 65

Listen and circle the best answer.

1. (a.) It's too heavy.
   b. It's too weak.

2. a. It's difficult.
   b. It's easy to follow.

3. a. The rug is too big.
   b. The rug is too small.

4. a. She needs more comfortable ones.
   b. She needs more powerful ones.

5. a. He doesn't want a fancy one.
   b. He wants a fancier one.

6. a. She wants a shorter one.
   b. She wants a longer one.

7. a. She wants a darker one.
   b. She wants a lighter one.

8. a. She'd like a fancier one.
   b. She wants to buy a more difficult one.

K. TICKETS CAN BE BOUGHT . . .

Student Course Book p. 66

Complete the sentence using *can be*.

1. I'd like to buy a ticket for the next flight to New York.

   Tickets for New York _____can be bought_____ on the airplane.

2. When should I pick up the cake that I ordered?

   Your cake _____ after 8:00 A.M.

3. Can I return this dress if it doesn't fit?

   All clothing _____ within ten days.

4. I want to send this package to Boston.

   How? Packages _____ first class or parcel post.

5. We'd like to see the apartment that's for rent.

   That apartment _____ tomorrow morning.

L. AT THE POST OFFICE

Student Course Book p. 66

1. I'm moving and need a _____.
   a. registered letter
   (b.) change of address form
   c. money order

2. I'd like to _____ a money order.
   a. file
   b. apply for
   c. buy

3. I have to get my mail from the _____.
   a. post office box
   b. first class stamps
   c. new forms

4. You can get stamps at the next _____.
   a. Window Number 3
   b. post office box
   c. window

5. Where can I _____ stamps?
   a. file
   b. apply for
   c. purchase

6. You can fill out this _____ over there.
   a. form
   b. box
   c. letter

M. IT'LL TAKE ABOUT TWO HOURS

Student Course Book p. 67

Fill in the blanks.

1. How long will it take to get to Baltimore?

    Let me see. To Baltimore from here . . . _____it'll take_____ about two hours.

2. When will you get your driver's license?

    I think _____ it next week.

3. What classes will your daughter take next semester?

    _____ biology and mathematics.

4. What do you think? When will Johnny get married?

    I think _____ married when he meets the right woman.

5. Where will your children go to school?

    _____ to the neighborhood school.

N. LISTENING

Student Course Book p. 67

Listen and circle the correct number.

1. (10) / 12
2. $20.96 / $12.96
3. seven / eleven
4. $14.68 / $40.68
5. five / nine
6. four / fourteen
7. $13.78 / $15.78
8. $10.64 / $12.64

O. IS OR ARE?

Student Course Book pp. 68–69

1. Taxes [is / (are)] included in the price.
2. Paychecks [is / are] given out every week.
3. The mail [is / are] picked up at noon.
4. Orders [is / are] taken over the phone.
5. Our computers [is / are] guaranteed.
6. This one [is / are] considered the best.
7. Payments [is / are] made monthly.
8. Our files [is / are] computerized.

P. APARTMENT HUNTING

Student Course Book pp. 68-69

Fill in the blank with the correct form.

Would you consider this to be a safe neighborhood?

　　This ____is considered___(1)___ one of the safest neighborhoods in the city.

Does the monthly fee include gas, electricity, parking, and security?

　　Yes.　All of those things _____(2)_____ in the monthly fee.

And do I make the payment at the beginning of the month?

　　All payments _____(3)_____ by the fifth of every month.

Do you charge a late fee?

　　Yes.　A fee of 10 percent _____(4)_____ after the sixth of every month.

Do you allow pets?

　　Cats and small dogs _____(5)_____.

Do you guarantee all the kitchen appliances?

　　The refrigerator, stove, and oven _____(6)_____.

Will you paint the apartment before you rent it?

　　Apartments _____(7)_____ before tenants move in.

Does the superintendent take care of problems quickly?

　　Problems _____(8)_____ care of as soon as possible.

How do you spell the superintendent's name?

　　His last name _____(9)_____ W-I-L-K-E-R-S-O-N.

Do you check references?

　　Yes.　All references _____(10)_____ carefully.

Where do I file my form?

　　All application forms _____(11)_____ at the rental office.

Could you please write down your telephone number for me?

　　Here is my business card.　My number _____(12)_____ on the card.

Q. **READING:** *Catalog Stores*   Student Course Book pp. 68-69

Shoppers in the United States have many different retail stores to choose from. They can shop at large department stores, furniture stores, jewelry stores, electronic equipment stores, clothing boutiques, and many others. Another type of retail store, the "catalog" store, has become popular with U.S. consumers.

Catalog stores offer much of the same merchandise as conventional retail stores. The catalogs are usually very big, and are filled with photographs and descriptions of all the different merchandise. The variety of products listed in the catalogs includes everything from appliances and baby clothing to video equipment and watches. The prices of these items are comparatively low. The same exact items often cost more in other retail stores.

When shoppers go to a catalog store, they see many brand-name products on display. If they are interested in purchasing an item, they need to follow a simple procedure. First, they go to a counter to find the store's catalog. They look in the catalog to find the exact item they wish to purchase. Then, they fill out an order form, which can usually be found on a shelf below the counter. The order form requires a lot of information: the name of the item, the item number found in the catalog, the price, and the customer's name and address. After completing the form, the customer gives it to a salesperson, who checks to see if the item is in stock. If the item is available, the stockroom sends it on a conveyor belt to the "pick-up" counter. When the item arrives at the pick-up counter, the customer's name is called and the customer pays for the item. The whole procedure usually takes ten to twenty minutes. If the item isn't available, the salesperson can usually check the store's computer and find out when it will be in stock again.

Catalog stores usually don't offer all the services that regular retail stores do. They usually don't have very many salespeople, and customers cannot expect to receive much assistance or attention from store employees. Customers need to know about the features and the quality of the items they wish to buy before they shop, since there is little opportunity to ask questions or examine the products in the store. However, catalog stores offer quality items at lower prices, and consumers seem to appreciate this.

I. TRUE or FALSE?   Put a T if the sentence is true, and F if it is false.

____ 1. A catalog store is a type of retail store.

____ 2. The items in catalog stores often cost more than items in other stores.

____ 3. In catalog stores, customers have to fill out order forms in order to purchase items.

____ 4. Customers at catalog stores use the store's computer to check the availability of items.

____ 5. Catalog stores are probably popular because the services they offer are excellent.

II. DID YOU UNDERSTAND?   Circle the correct answer.

1. "Consumers" in this reading passage means _____.
   a. salespeople
   b. shoppers
   c. services

2. Another word for "merchandise" is _____.
   a. products
   b. photographs
   c. clothing

3. "In stock" in this reading passage means _____.
   a. in the catalog
   b. at the pick-up counter
   c. available

4. The customer finds the item number _____.
   a. on the order form
   b. on the shelf below the counter
   c. in the catalog

5. The most important idea of the passage is that catalog stores _____.
   a. offer quality merchandise at lower prices
   b. are more popular than conventional retail stores
   c. offer the exact item the customer wishes to purchase

A. **HAVE YOU EVER . . . ?**   Student Course Book pp. 72–73

Complete the question and the answer.

1. __Have__ you ever used a credit card?
   Yes, __I have__.

2. _____ he ever driven a bus?
   No, _____.

3. _____ they ever gone to Italy?
   No, _____.

4. _____ it ever snowed in Mexico?
   Yes, _____.

5. _____ she ever made Chinese food?
   No, _____.

6. _____ Ms. Smith ever been late?
   Yes, _____.

7. _____ you ever eaten squid?
   No, _____.

8. _____ Joe ever gotten a speeding ticket?
   Yes, _____.

B. **WHICH WORD?**   Student Course Book pp. 72-73

Circle the best answer.

1. Please _____ the slip on this line.
   a. use
   (b.) sign
   c. prepare

2. _____ a little wax on the table.
   a. Pour
   b. Polish
   c. Twist

3. _____ the papers into small pieces.
   a. Press
   b. Type
   c. Cut up

4. He _____ the box on the floor.
   a. placed
   b. put in
   c. called

5. You can _____ it out of here.
   a. put
   b. handle
   c. take

6. _____ in here to turn it on.
   a. Place
   b. Press
   c. Take

7. I _____ cheese on top of my tacos.
   a. whip
   b. put
   c. twist

8. Push down the top of the medicine bottle and then _____ it to the left.
   a. make
   b. knit
   c. twist

70

C. **JOBS** Student Course Book pp. 72-73

> use this polishing machine   use this typewriter
> use the credit card machine   start this computer
> verify this credit card   polish the car

1. Could you show me how to _start this computer_ ?
   Sure. First, press this button and the screen will light up.

2. Could you tell me how to _____?
   Certainly. Place the card and the charge slip in the machine.

3. Could you show me how to _____?
   Of course. Call this telephone number and tell them the account number.

4. Could you tell me how to _____?
   Yes. Apply the wax, let it dry, and then remove it with a dry cloth.

5. Could you show me how to _____?
   Sure. Be sure you flip this switch. Set the margins with these keys.

6. Could you demonstrate how to _____?
   Of course. Spray the wax, turn it on here, and use a back-and-forth motion like this.

D. **WHICH WORD DOESN'T BELONG?** Student Course Book pp. 72–73

1. *spray:*   water   wax   hair spray   (paper)
2. *take off:* sweater   hat   cover   supervisor
3. *pour:*   bulb   sauce   coffee   syrup
4. *set:*   margins   table   clock   sofa
5. *sign:*   paycheck   stop   lease   contract

E. **MATCHING** Student Course Book pp. 74-75

1. Attach ⎯⎯⎯⎯⎯⎯⎯⎯⎯⎯⎯⎯⎯⎯⎯⎯⎯ the original paper face down.
2. Detach ⎯⎯⎯⎯⎯⎯⎯⎯⎯⎯⎯⎯⎯⎯⎯⎯⎯ the new ribbon to the empty spool.
3. Place   the wires from the back of the stereo.

4. Use this bottle to   verify the credit card.
5. Call this number to   flip the switch.
6. The machine will start when you   spray the windows.

7. Check to make sure   "hold."
8. Dial the   extension.
9. Put the caller on   it's working.

10. Put the letter face down   in the basement.
11. The supplies are down   the side of the machine.
12. The copies come out   on the glass.

F. FIRST DAY ON THE JOB

Student Course Book pp. 74–75

| make | take | answer | check | call |

1. Please ____make____ sure there's enough coffee.
2. Do you think you could _____ the phones?
3. Can you _____ these reports for mistakes?
4. _____ a message if Mr. Wilson calls.
5. Could you _____ the airline and make my plane reservations?

G. LISTENING

Student Course Book pp. 74–75

Listen and decide what they're talking about. Circle the best answer.

1. a. a typewriter
   b. a light bulb
   c. a polishing machine

2. a. setting margins
   b. making copies
   c. opening office doors

3. a. replacing a typewriter ribbon
   b. registering at a new school
   c. learning to swim

4. a. a copying machine
   b. a soda machine
   c. a broken hose

5. a. setting up a stereo
   b. calling for an appointment
   c. transferring a call

6. a. a VCR
   b. a toaster oven
   c. an engine tune-up

H. COULD YOU TELL ME HOW?

Student Course Book pp. 74–75

Circle the best response.

1. Could you tell me how?
   a. I follow you.
   b. I'd be glad to.
   c. Repeat it.

2. Could you please repeat that?
   a. I'm afraid I don't know how.
   b. Okay.
   c. You've got it.

3. Could I ask you to help?
   a. Let me see if I understand.
   b. Certainly. I'd be happy to.
   c. You've already helped me.

4. Let me know if you have any questions.
   a. I will.
   b. I see.
   c. I missed.

5. Have you got that?
   a. I'm glad.
   b. I'm following you.
   c. I get that.

6. Are you with me so far?
   a. I'm close to you.
   b. Let's go.
   c. Yes.

7. Be sure to turn the machine off.
   a. I'm sure.
   b. I will.
   c. Tell me.

8. How's the job going?
   a. I'm glad.
   b. I see.
   c. Very well.

I. HE DREW UP THE CONTRACT Student Course Book p. 76

1. [He drew up / He's drawn up] the contract this morning.

2. [Has / Did] the new mechanic ever put together an engine before?

3. This is the first time [she's written out / she wrote out] an accident report.

4. What time [have they left / did they leave] the airport?

5. The new clerks [have never taken / never took] inventory before.

J. DID YOU FINISH? Student Course Book p. 76

did   have   has

1. __Did__ you finish?
   Yes, we __did__.

2. _____ the boss left?
   Yes, she _____.

3. _____ he fill out the report?
   Yes, he _____.

4. _____ they gone on strike?
   Yes, they _____.

5. _____ it started to snow?
   Yes, it _____.

6. _____ you and Bob miss the flight?
   Yes, we _____.

7. _____ your parents gotten a new car yet?
   Yes, they _____.

8. _____ the motor break down?
   Yes, it _____.

K. DID YOU TAKE OUT THE TRASH? Student Course Book p. 76

up   out   on   in   off

1. Did you take __out__ the trash?
2. They've already drawn _____ the lease.
3. It's hot! Take _____ your coat.
4. Cut _____ the vegetables into small pieces.
5. I'm going to try this dress _____.
6. She hung _____ on me!
7. Have you filled _____ the application form yet?
8. Press _____ to turn the machine on.
9. Throw _____ all your old papers.
10. Put these files _____ the drawer.

73

L. I'VE ALREADY FILLED IT OUT

Student Course Book p. 76

Complete the sentence.

1. Please fill out this application.

   I've already __filled it out__.

2. I've got to put together all these pieces.

   I'll help you _____.

3. Did the personnel officer draw up your employment contract?

   He _____ this morning.

4. I don't know how to take up these pants.

   I'll show you how to _____ in a few minutes.

5. When are you going to write out the answers to the questions?

   I'll _____ this weekend.

6. Could I ask you to set up the room?

   I _____ yesterday.

7. Who's going to throw out the trash?

   I _____ a few minutes ago.

8. Write out the names of all your children on this insurance form.

   There's not enough space to _____ _____!

M. SHE WAS GOING TO TAKE IT UP . . .

Student Course Book p. 77

Complete the sentence using *was going to* or *were going to*.

1. Did your mother take up the hem on your new dress?

   No, she didn't. She __was going to take it up__ last night, but she got a headache.

2. Is Michael going to the party tomorrow night?

   No, he isn't. He _____, but he has to finish a term paper.

3. Have you filled out your time sheet yet?

   No, I haven't. I _____ tomorrow morning.

4. Have the repairmen come to fix the copying machine?

   No, not yet. They _____ this morning, but they got delayed.

5. When do you plan to leave for your vacation?

   We _____ on Monday, but we had to change our plans.

6. Have you taken your medicine today?

   No, I haven't. I _____ after lunch.

N. BUT ...

Student Course Book p. 77

Complete the sentence using *supposed to*.

1. Let's take the trash out tomorrow morning.

    But the trash ___is supposed to be taken out___ tonight!

2. We'll polish the floors in the hallway after the break.

    But the floors _____ right now!

3. Can you give out the mail after lunch?

    But the mail _____ *before* lunch!

4. I'll type these reports on Monday morning.

    But these reports _____ today!

5. We're going to hand in our term papers next week.

    But the term papers _____ *this* week!

6. I set the table for eight people.

    But the table _____ for *ten* people!

7. We just gave the dog three cans of food.

    But the dog _____ only *one* can of food!

8. I'd like to eat dessert now.

    But dessert _____ *after* you eat your dinner!

O. MATCHING

Student Course Book p. 78

Where is the best place to find these things? Write the correct letter.

_b_ 1. napkins   a. employee lounge

___ 2. paychecks   b. cafeteria

___ 3. soda machine   c. Accounting Department

___ 4. application forms   d. Personnel Office

___ 5. conveyor belt   e. stockroom

___ 6. typewriter ribbons f. assembly line

75

P. FIRST DAY ON THE JOB   Student Course Book p. 78

> Where is his office?   I don't know **where his office is**.
> Which shelf are they on?   I don't know **which shelf they're on**.
>
> What does he look like?   I don't know **what he looks like**.
> Which one do you mean?   I don't know **which one you mean**.

Complete the sentence.

1. Excuse me. Where is gate 9?

    I don't know _where gate 9 is._

2. When are they going to arrive?

    I'm not sure _____

3. Where's she from?

    I have no idea _____

4. Why do they always come late?

    I don't know _____

5. Which floor does James work on?

    I'm not sure _____

6. What kind of sauce is that?

    I don't know _____

7. Who are they looking for?

    I don't know _____

8. How's Fred doing?

    I have no idea _____

9. Where are the elevators?

    I don't know _____

10. Who's that?

    I'm not sure _____

11. Where am I supposed to take these boxes?

    I don't know _____

12. Why does this car cost so much?

    I have no idea _____

Q. I'M NOT CERTAIN

Student Course Book p. 78

Circle the best answer.

1. I'm not certain _____.
   a. which floor he works on *(circled)*
   b. which floor does he work on
   c. which is the floor he works on

2. She doesn't remember _____.
   a. where is the car parked
   b. where the car is parked
   c. the car where it is parked

3. They've forgotten _____.
   a. what is his telephone number
   b. what his telephone number is
   c. what it is his telephone number

4. Brenda isn't sure _____.
   a. what is she going to do
   b. what's she going to do
   c. what she's going to do

5. We have no idea _____.
   a. what time they're coming
   b. when are they coming
   c. what time are they coming

6. I think I know _____.
   a. which car does she like best
   b. which car she does like best
   c. which car she likes best

7. You need to find out _____.
   a. how much does it cost
   b. how much it costs
   c. how much it does cost

8. Ask your supervisor _____.
   a. when you get your first paycheck
   b. when do you get your first paycheck
   c. when you do get your first paycheck

R. WHAT'S THE CORRECT WORD?

Student Course Book p. 79

Circle the best answer.

1. _____ are supposed to be submitted by noon today.
   a. Employees
   b. Deductions
   c. Time sheets *(circled)*

2. He hopes to be _____ for a raise after one year.
   a. required
   b. eligible
   c. in effect

3. That's your Social Security _____.
   a. salary
   b. employment
   c. deduction

4. You receive ten _____ days a year.
   a. medical
   b. pension
   c. sick

5. Does the company have _____ plan?
   a. a pension
   b. an employment
   c. a salary

6. Your raise took _____ last month.
   a. taxes and deductions
   b. effect
   c. a promotion

7. This deduction is for _____.
   a. medical insurance
   b. your paycheck
   c. employment

8. Your _____ is required to sign your time sheet.
   a. signature
   b. paycheck
   c. supervisor

S. COULD YOU TELL ME . . . ?

Student Course Book p. 79

Where **is** the bank?	Could you tell me **where the bank is**?
When **will** I receive it?	Could you tell me **when I'll receive it**?
What **does** he look like?	Could you tell me **what he looks like**?
Where **did** Mr. Bell go?	Could you tell me **where Mr. Bell went**?

Complete the question.

1. (Where is the bank?)

   Could you tell me ___where the bank is?___

2. (When will I be able to take a break?)

   Would you know _____

3. (How many letters do I have to type?)

   Can you please tell me _____

4. (Why did they deduct so many taxes?)

   Do you by any chance know _____

5. (Where's the ladies' room?)

   Could you please tell me _____

6. (What did the boss say at the meeting?)

   Would you by any chance know _____

7. (When do the benefits take effect?)

   Could you possibly tell me _____

T. DO YOU HAPPEN TO KNOW . . . ?

Student Course Book p. 79

Circle the best answer.

1. Do you happen to know _____?
   a. what time is it
   (b.) what time it is
   c. what's the time

2. Would you know _____?
   a. where's Oak Street
   b. where is Oak Street
   c. where Oak Street is

3. Could you tell me _____?
   a. Ms. Temple who is she
   b. who Ms. Temple is
   c. who is Ms. Temple

4. Can you tell me _____?
   a. when does the bus come
   b. the bus when it comes
   c. when the bus comes

5. Do you have any idea _____?
   a. where I punch in
   b. where do I punch in
   c. where I do punch in

6. Could you please show me _____?
   a. where is the lounge located
   b. where the lounge it is located
   c. where the lounge is located

U. DO YOU KNOW IF...?

Student Course Book p. 80

> Are ties required?   Do you know **if/whether ties are required**?
> Do we need these glasses?   Do you know **if/whether we need these glasses**?

Write an appropriate question for Speaker A.

1. A. Are we expected to punch out for our break?
   B. I don't know. You should ask Alice.
   A. Alice, do you know if _we're expected to punch out for our break?_

2. A. Do we have to wear gloves?
   B. I have no idea. Check with Brad.
   A. Brad, can you tell us whether _____

3. A. Does the boss insist on hairnets?
   B. I'm not sure. Ask Susan.
   A. Susan, would you happen to know if _____

4. A. Is this standard procedure?
   B. I'm not certain. Let's ask Jeff.
   A. Jeff, do you by any chance know whether _____

5. A. Are we required to work overtime?
   B. I don't know. You should ask Mrs. Vann.
   A. Mrs. Vann, could you tell us if _____

6. A. Am I eligible for the contest?
   B. I'm not sure. Let's check with Tracy.
   A. Tracy, do you happen to know whether _____

V. WHICH IS THE SAME?

Student Course Book p. 80

Circle the answer that is *closest in meaning*.

1. Am I eligible for the pension plan?
   a. Can you tell me when I am eligible for the pension plan?
   b. Would you know if I am eligible for the pension plan?
   c. Could you tell me whether you are eligible for the pension plan?

2. When is it necessary to punch out?
   a. Do you happen to know if we have to punch out?
   b. Would you tell me if it is necessary to punch out?
   c. Can you tell me when we have to punch out?

3. Are these deductions mandatory?
   a. Could you tell me if we must have these deductions?
   b. Do you happen to know why these deductions are mandatory?
   c. Do you by any chance know how many deductions we have to have?

4. Where are we supposed to leave our jackets?
   a. Can you tell me when we're supposed to wear our jackets?
   b. Would you happen to know where we should leave our jackets?
   c. Do you know whether we're supposed to leave our jackets?

79

W. ARE YOU WITH ME SO FAR?

Student Course Book p. 80

1. _____ so far?
   a. If you are with me
   b. Do you be with me
   c. Are you with me

2. _____ the account number?
   a. Could you by any chance know
   b. Would you happen to know
   c. Can I ask you whether

3. Is it _____?
   a. requirement
   b. need
   c. essential

4. Could you possibly _____?
   a. happen to ask the boss
   b. ask the boss
   c. please ask the boss

5. I asked _____ time I had a question.
   a. all the
   b. every single
   c. some

6. Do you think you could _____?
   a. help us
   b. happen to help me
   c. supposed to help

7. Am I really _____ to make coffee?
   a. expecting
   b. have
   c. supposed

8. It's our _____ to help.
   a. necessary
   b. policy
   c. regulation

X. WAS IT DIFFICULT FOR YOU . . . ?

Student Course Book p. 81

> I / He / She / We / You / They **had given** demonstrations before.
>
> I / He / She / We / You / They **hadn't given** speeches before.

Complete the answer.

1. Was it difficult for you to make the sales presentation?

   No. _____*I had made*_____ sales presentations before.

2. Did he have trouble using the copying machine?

   Yes. _____*He hadn't used*_____ a copying machine before.

3. Did they have a hard time filling out their time sheets?

   Yes. _____ time sheets before.

4. Did you have any trouble putting together the motor?

   No. _____ a lot of motors at my previous job.

5. Did Mrs. Wood have trouble writing out the accident report?

   No. _____ many accident reports before.

6. Was Sheila having difficulty changing the typewriter ribbon?

   Yes. _____ a typewriter ribbon before.

Y. I HADN'T STUDIED ...

Student Course Book p. 81

Circle the best answer.

1. _____ English before I came to this school.
   a. I have studied
   (b.) I hadn't studied
   c. I'm studying

2. They _____ met before.
   a. aren't
   b. didn't
   c. had

3. She _____ a headache before she got to the party.
   a. had had
   b. has had
   c. has

4. Because we _____ prepared well, we did well.
   a. had
   b. did
   c. have

5. We enjoyed working there because the job _____ so interesting.
   a. had been
   b. is
   c. has been

6. I _____ a teacher for ten years before I became a lawyer.
   a. am
   b. have been
   c. had been

7. Previously, the company _____ taxes from our paychecks.
   a. had only deducted
   b. has only deducted
   c. only deducts

8. It was easy since _____.
   a. she hadn't done it before
   b. she had done it before
   c. she's doing it well

Z. DO YOU HAVE ANY QUESTIONS?

Student Course Book p. 81

Circle the sentence that is *closest in meaning*.

1. Do you have any questions?
   (a.) Could you tell me if you have any questions?
   b. Can you please have any questions?
   c. Do you know the questions?

2. Where's the file?
   a. Would you know if there's a file?
   b. Do you happen to know where the file is?
   c. Can you tell me where's the file?

3. Is he having trouble?
   a. Do you know he's having trouble?
   b. Would he happen to have trouble?
   c. Could you possibly tell me if he's having trouble?

4. When do we get to go to lunch?
   a. Would you know when we got to lunch?
   b. Do you happen to know when we get to go to lunch?
   c. Can you please tell us what time we went to lunch?

5. Why did the supervisor leave early?
   a. Would you happen to know why the supervisor left early?
   b. Could you possibly ask why the supervisor left early?
   c. Do you have any idea why the supervisor leaves early?

6. Was the test difficult?
   a. Would you by any chance know the test was difficult?
   b. Did you happen to know was the test difficult?
   c. Can you tell me whether the test was difficult?

| AA. | **WITH SUGAR AND A LITTLE CREAM** | Student Course Book p. 81 |

For each dialog, circle the correct line for Speaker A.

1. A.   a. Do you know whether he likes coffee?
   - (b.) Would you happen to know how he likes his coffee?
   - c. Can you tell me who likes coffee?

   B. With sugar and a little cream.

2. A.   a. Could you tell me why we have to wear helmets?
   - b. Can you please tell me if we need to wear helmets?
   - c. Do you happen to know when it's essential to wear helmets?

   B. Because it's a safety rule.

3. A.   a. Would you by any chance know where the secretary is?
   - b. Could you please hand out the paychecks this afternoon?
   - c. I'd like you to take these boxes to the supply room.

   B. I'm not sure where it is.

4. A.   a. Are you having trouble with your time sheet?
   - b. Do you feel you've "got the hang of it"?
   - c. We're pleased to have you "on board."

   B. Yes. I've learned a lot this week.

5. A.   a. Do you happen to know if anything else is supposed to be done?
   - b. Please don't hesitate to let me know if you have any problems.
   - c. I really don't want to bother you, but I have a question.

   B. No, I don't think so.

6. A.   a. May I please ask a question?
   - b. I'd be happy to show you how.
   - c. I don't think you did that quite right.

   B. Hmm. Could you please show me how?

7. A.   a. I'd like you to ask a favor.
   - b. Could I please ask you a favor?
   - c. Can you please ask a favor?

   B. Certainly. How can I help?

8. A.   a. Is it mandatory that we wear these glasses?
   - b. Did you see where I left my glasses?
   - c. It's a regulation that we wear these glasses.

   B. Oh. I see.

9. A.   a. I was planning to make some coffee in a few minutes.
   - b. Have you ever made coffee before?
   - c. So how do you like your coffee?

   B. I thought you made it already.

BB.   READING: *John Wood's First Day on the Job*   Student Course Book p. 81

John Wood started a new job today at the Webster Computer Company. It was a very busy day! In his first hours at the office this morning, the secretary introduced John to about twenty people: the boss, the supervisors, and many of the employees. The secretary told John the job title of each employee and the name of each employee's department. John couldn't believe all the information he was hearing: first names, last names, job titles, departments! "How will I ever remember all of this?" he thought to himself.

Next, John had to go to the Personnel Department to fill out some forms. The Personnel Officer had a lot of questions: "Do you know how many tax deductions you want taken out of your paycheck? Have you decided which health insurance plan you want? Would you like the dental plan? How about the pension plan?" John couldn't make all the decisions right away, so the Personnel Officer gave him some information to take home. He'll have to return in a few days with his decisions and complete the forms.

John went back to his department and was ready to learn all about his new job. But every time he tried to get started, he had to stop and ask for something. "Could you please tell me where the supplies are?" "Would you please show me how I start this copying machine?" "How do I transfer this call?" After a while, he needed to take a break. "Can you tell me where I can get a cup of coffee?" "Is there an employee lounge?" "Would you please tell me where the bathroom is?" At lunch time, he had even more questions. "How long is the lunch break?" "Do you know a good place to eat?"

John had so much information to learn, so many decisions to make, and so many questions to ask that he felt overwhelmed at the end of the first day. But he also felt very lucky to have such patient and understanding co-workers who would help him through the next few weeks.

I. TRUE or FALSE?   Put a T if the sentence is true, and F if it is false.

____   1.   John was very busy on his first day on the job.

____   2.   He had trouble answering the Personnel Officer's questions.

____   3.   He was able to transfer a call without help.

____   4.   John works in the Personnel Department.

____   5.   He probably thought that his first day on the job was very difficult.

II. DID YOU UNDERSTAND?   Circle the correct answer.

1. John probably took the job _____.
    a. to learn about copying machines
    b. to learn about computers
    c. to understand insurance plans

2. The Personnel Officer probably gave John _____.
    a. his first paycheck
    b. information about other employees
    c. explanations of insurance plans

3. John probably felt _____ at the end of his first day.
    a. tired
    b. important
    c. desirable

4. At the end of the first day of work, John _____ his co-workers.
    a. excused
    b. knew
    c. appreciated

5. John felt overwhelmed because _____.
    a. his first day had been so busy
    b. he had to go to the Personnel Department
    c. he had such helpful co-workers

9

A. I DON'T FEEL LIKE ...
Student Course Book p. 84

| drive | go | play | see | take | do |

I don't want to { **play** tennis. / **go** to the movies. / **have** a picnic. }

I don't feel like { **playing** tennis. / **going** to the movies. / **having** a picnic. }

Complete the conversation and practice with another student.

Do you want to ___go___₁ swimming?

No, I don't feel like _____₂ swimming today.

How about _____₃ to the mountains?

No, I'm not really in the mood to _____₄ anywhere.

What about a movie? Would you like to _____₅ "The Shark"?

No, I really don't want to _____₆ a movie.

Do you feel like _____₇ soccer?

No, I don't want to _____₈ soccer.

Well, what do you want to _____₉?

I guess I don't feel like _____₁₀ anything!

B. THEY'VE PLAYED TENNIS FOR THE PAST TWO YEARS
Student Course Book p. 84

1. Are your kids going to play tennis this summer?

   Probably. ___They've played___ tennis for the past two years.

2. Does your husband still work at the factory?

   No, he doesn't. ___He hasn't worked___ there since last year.

3. Will Chris be at the pool tomorrow?

   Yes, she probably will. _____ at the pool every day this week.

4. Did you go skating at the pond last weekend?

   No, we didn't. Actually, _____ skating there for a long time.

5. Does Martin Shore still live here?

   No. _____ here for a long time.

84

C. HOW ABOUT GOING TO THE LAKE?

Student Course Book p. 85

| How about / What about / Do you feel like | **going** to the lake? | I want to / I'd like to / I'd prefer to / I'd rather | **go** to the pool. |

Circle the correct words and practice the conversation with another student.

What would you like [doing / (to do)]¹ tonight?

Oh, I don't know. Do you feel like [to see / seeing]² a movie? We could always [go / going]³ to the new theater at the mall.

I think I'd prefer [staying / to stay]⁴ home tonight. How about [to get / getting]⁵ a videocassette from the VCR Club?

Okay. Are you in the mood [to watch / watching]⁶ a comedy?

Hmm. I'd rather [get / getting]⁷ a mystery.

That's fine. It really doesn't matter to me.

D. WHY DON'T WE GO FOR A HIKE?

Student Course Book p. 85

1. Why don't we go for a [(hike) / bike]?
2. We could play "hide and [see / seek]."
3. How about swimming [to the pool / at the pond]?
4. I'd rather [prefer / play] hopscotch.
5. I'd like to [visit / do] a museum.
6. Let's go skating [on the lake / at the pool].
7. What about [hiking / riding] our bikes?
8. We've just seen an adventure [museum / film].

85

E. **DO YOU WANT TO GO SWIMMING?**   Student Course Book p. 86

> Would you like to
> How would you like to } take a ride?   Would you be interested in **taking** a ride?
> Do you want to

1. Do you want to _____?
   a. going swimming
   b. swimming
   (c.) go swimming

2. How would you like _____?
   a. to go ski
   b. going skiing
   c. to go skiing

3. Would you like to _____?
   a. taking a ride
   b. take a ride
   c. riding

4. Is he interested in _____?
   a. doing extra work
   b. do extra work
   c. does extra work

5. Would you be interested in _____?
   a. skate
   b. go skating
   c. going skating

6. Do you want _____?
   a. play golf
   b. to play golf
   c. to play golfing

7. They're interested in _____.
   a. play outdoors
   b. played outdoors
   c. playing outdoors

8. Does he feel like _____?
   a. to have a picnic
   b. having a picnic
   c. he has a picnic

F. **TAKING A RIDE IS A GREAT IDEA!**   Student Course Book p. 86

> **Taking** a ride is a great idea!

1. I'd like to play football, but my parents think that ___*playing*___ soccer is a better idea.

2. She really wants to take ballet lessons, but _____ lessons from a professional is so expensive!

3. We'd like to go sailing, but _____ sailing with the kids wouldn't be a good idea.

4. I'd really like to drive that sports car, but _____ a car with a manual transmission is too difficult for me.

5. I understand why we have to wear protective clothing, but _____ these glasses is really uncomfortable.

6. They want to ride their bikes, but I told them that _____ on the highway is too dangerous.

7. I know that they have to deduct taxes, but _____ $150.00 from every paycheck is too much!

8. I like to drink coffee in the morning, but _____ more than one cup makes me nervous.

9. My teenage daughters want to hang out at the shopping mall, but I think _____ at the mall isn't a good idea.

G. LISTENING

Student Course Book p. 86

Listen to the weather forecast and circle the sentence that is true.

1. a. It's supposed to be clear this afternoon.
   (b.) It's supposed to rain.

2. a. It's 45 degrees right now.
   b. It's 30 degrees right now.

3. a. It's supposed to snow this morning.
   b. It's supposed to rain this morning.

4. a. It'll be in the 80s tonight.
   b. It'll be in the 70s tonight.

5. a. It's supposed to be foggy.
   b. It's supposed to rain in the area.

6. a. It's going to be sunny today.
   b. It's going to be windy today.

H. HOW WOULD YOU LIKE . . . ?

Student Course Book p. 87

Circle the best answer.

1. How would you like _____?
   a. go swimming
   (b.) to go swimming
   c. swimming

2. Are you in the mood _____?
   a. to dance
   b. dancing
   c. dance

3. I'm interested in _____.
   a. skiing
   b. to ski
   c. to going skiing

4. I think she'd prefer _____.
   a. take the bus
   b. to taking the bus
   c. to take the bus

5. I'd like you _____.
   a. playing outdoors.
   b. to play outdoors.
   c. played outdoors.

6. We're supposed _____.
   a. studying for a test.
   b. to study for a test.
   c. study for a test.

7. George didn't feel like _____.
   a. left
   b. to leave
   c. leaving

8. They'd rather _____.
   a. to go sailing
   b. going sailing
   c. go sailing

I. LOIS WON'T BE ABLE TO ATTEND THE MEETING

Student Course Book p. 87

Circle the best answer.

1. Lois _____ to attend the meeting.
   a. supposed
   b. can't
   (c.) won't be able

2. We had _____ our homework.
   a. finish
   b. got to finish
   c. to finish

3. James _____ work overtime.
   a. won't be able
   b. can't
   c. have to

4. _____ they supposed to come?
   a. Are
   b. Did
   c. Will

5. _____ got to take a taxi.
   a. She'll
   b. She's
   c. She'd

6. _____ be able to arrive on time?
   a. Are they
   b. Do they
   c. Will they

J. ORDERING

Student Course Book p. 88

Draw a line to the correct words for each group.

1. Let me have five pieces of — coffee.
2. Give me a cup of — french fries.
3. I'll take an order of — chicken.

4. May I — for anything else?
5. Would you care — two?
6. Would you like — help you?

7. I'd like an order of — go.
8. I'll have a — refried beans.
9. This is to — shake.

K. I'D LIKE A FOOTBALL

Student Course Book p. 88

Complete the response.

1. What do you want for your birthday?

   _____I'd like_____ a football.

2. Which flavor does he care for?

   _____ chocolate.

   > I'd
   > He'd
   > She'd } **like** a hamburger.
   > We'd
   > They'd

3. What can I get for you?

   _____ some napkins for our children.

4. What would they like for dessert?

   _____ fresh fruit.

5. What does Mrs. Warren want?

   _____ another cup of tea.

6. Which bike would your son prefer?

   _____ the red one.

L. MORE FOOD

Student Course Book p. 89

Circle the best answer.

1. Would you care for a glass _____?
   a. of beans
   b. Pepsi
   (c.) of iced tea

2. I'll have the _____ ribs.
   a. creamy
   b. thousand
   c. barbecued

3. I prefer _____ juice.
   a. carrot
   b. tofu
   c. milk

4. I'd rather have a baked _____.
   a. vegetarian
   b. potato
   c. bean

5. Do you have _____ meals?
   a. mashed
   b. vegetarian
   c. iced

6. Do you want to try the _____ loaf?
   a. bread
   b. creamy
   c. meat

M. LISTENING

Student Course Book p. 89

Listen and circle the correct response.

1. a. Yes, I would.
   b. We'd like to.
   (c.) I'll have carrot juice.

2. a. Salad and soup.
   b. I'd prefer a salad.
   c. I think I would.

3. a. With what kind of dressing?
   b. Red or white?
   c. Do you want something to drink with that?

4. a. My wife.
   b. We'll be very careful.
   c. A cup of tea.

5. a. Sorry. We don't have any tofu.
   b. Okay. Are you ready to order?
   c. And would you care for some tofu?

6. a. May I help you?
   b. That's right.
   c. Is that for here or to go?

N. THE TACOS ARE WONDERFUL

Student Course Book p. 90

| is | a few | it |
| are | a little | them |

1. The tacos ____are____ wonderful. Could I possibly have _____ more?
2. Would you care for _____ more rolls? I can get _____ right away.
3. Could we have _____ more butter? We need _____ for our baked potatoes.
4. I have _____ more mushrooms left, but I don't think I can finish _____.
5. This chili _____ fantastic. Would you like to try _____?
6. How _____ everything? Would you care for _____ more wine?

O. AT A RESTAURANT

Student Course Book p. 90

Complete the conversation using *few* or *little* and practice with another student.

Hello. I'm the owner of the restaurant. How's your dinner this evening?

    The pizza we ordered is delicious!

Well, I'm really glad you like it. It's my special recipe. First, I put a ____little____ tomato sauce
                                                                              1
on the pizza dough. Then I place a _____ pieces of eggplant on top. Then I add a
                                          2
_____ slices of ham and sprinkle a _____ cheese on top. I put it in the oven
      3   4
for just a _____ minutes. I don't like to overcook it.
                5

    Well, it's wonderful!

Thank you. Can I get anything else for you? Would you care for a _____ more wine?
                                                                        6

    No, thanks. We were just planning to get a _____ more salad from the salad bar.
                                                              7

Well, enjoy your meal, folks!

P. BUYING TICKETS

Student Course Book p. 91

1. We don't have any seats left in _____.
   a. this evening's performance
   b. Saturday
   (c.) the balcony

2. How much _____ the tickets be?
   a. are
   b. do
   c. would

3. Tonight's _____ is sold out.
   a. balcony
   b. performance
   c. orchestra

4. How much are they _____?
   a. be
   b. apiece
   c. left

5. Are there any tickets available for today's _____?
   a. match
   b. mezzanine
   c. grandstand

6. I have seats in the _____.
   a. concert
   b. bleachers
   c. level

7. I'll take two tickets for today's _____.
   a. section
   b. orchestra
   c. matinee

8. The _____ was wonderful!
   a. superb
   b. orchestra
   c. tonight

Q. LISTENING

Student Course Book p. 91

Listen and complete the sentence.

how	who

1. (a.) much it'll cost.
   b. is going to come.

rice	ice

2. a. in your drink?
   b. with your chicken?

fries	size

3. a. isn't in stock.
   b. will be ready soon.

shops	chops

4. a. are delicious!
   b. are closed on Mondays.

seat	heat

5. a. in the balcony cost?
   b. in your apartment cost?

care	wear

6. a. this tie to work?
   b. for a cup of coffee?

Jane's	jeans

7. a. books?
   b. on sale?

Peas	Please

8. a. answer the phone for me.
   b. are in the Produce Section.

wrecked	checked

9. a. my brand new car!
   b. the report for mistakes.

features	bleachers

10. a. are included with this car?
    b. have the best view?

R. LISTENING

Student Course Book p. 91

Listen and circle the correct answer.

1. ⓐ. He paid $3.00 each.
   b. He bought three tickets.

2. a. He purchased five tickets.
   b. There weren't any seats left in the grandstand.

3. a. The man is interested in buying three tickets.
   b. He wants to buy six tickets.

4. a. There will be no concert tonight.
   b. The concert is sold out.

5. a. He can get seats in Section T.
   b. There are some seats in Section G.

6. a. He paid $10.00.
   b. He paid $20.00.

7. a. The man wanted upper level seats.
   b. The man wanted ground level seats.

8. a. They're going to tonight's performance.
   b. They got seats for the matinee.

S. MOVIES

Student Course Book p. 92

Match the movie title in the first column with the types of movies in the second column.

_b_ 1. *A Million Laughs*   a. a mystery

___ 2. *Korea Today*   b. a comedy

___ 3. *A Journey to Mars*   c. a documentary

___ 4. *Una Vita Speciale*   d. a children's film

___ 5. *Who Did It?*   e. a western

___ 6. *Baby Bear Goes to the Zoo*   f. a science fiction movie

___ 7. *Cowboy Jones*   g. a foreign film

T. LISTENING: *Theater Information*

Student Course Book p. 92

What movies are playing?   Call the movie theater and listen to the recordings.

Listen to the first recording.   Then answer these questions.

1. What time is the first show?
   a. At 6:45.
   ⓑ. At 7:30.

2. How many shows are there?
   a. Three.
   b. Two.

3. How much does it cost for each ticket?
   a. $4.00.
   b. $3.00.

Listen to the second recording.   Then answer these questions.

4. What's the name of the movie at the Town Theater?
   a. *We Are Happy.*
   b. *The Friendly Giant.*

5. How many times a day do they show the movie?
   a. Once.
   b. Three times.

6. How much are the tickets for the 5:00 show?
   a. $6.00 each.
   b. $3.00 each.

U. WHAT'S ON?

Student Course Book p. 93

Write the correct answer.

1. What channel should you turn to if you want to watch the news?

   __Channel 4__

2. Which program is a documentary?
   _____

3. Which program is probably part of a miniseries?
   _____

4. Which program is probably a game show?
   _____

5. Which program at 7:00 is probably a children's show?
   _____

6. Which program is probably a police show?
   _____

7. Which channel do teenagers probably watch every week at 7:30?
   _____

7:00 PM

- **2** HEALTH CLUBS IN AMERICA. A Special Report.
- **4** NEWS WITH RICHARD FLANIGAN. National and international news.
- **7** TRY YOUR LUCK.
- **9** ZAZA, THE POWER PRINCESS. Zaza fights a big battle against Thor.

7:30 PM

- **4** GROWING UP IN THE CITY. Richard has a problem and goes to his parents for help. Part 3.
- **7** SOUNDS GOOD. A countdown of the top ten music videos of the week.
- **9** DETECTIVE DRAKE. Drake solves a difficult case with the help of an old friend.

---

8. How long is the news program?
   _____

9. Which program is on for one hour?
   _____

V. MATCHING

Student Course Book p. 93

Draw a line to the correct words for each group.

1. I'm not in the mood to watch a situation — show.
2. I'd rather watch a game — opera.
3. I'm tired of watching that soap — comedy.

4. I don't   any difference to me.
5. It doesn't   matter to me.
6. It doesn't make   care.

7. What's on   8:00?
8. What's on at   Channel 7?
9. Why don't we look in   the TV listings?

W. **READING:** *Videocassette Recorders*

  The way that many people in the United States watch movies has changed in recent years. People don't just "go to the movies" any more, they also take the movies home! The videocassette recorder has made this possible, and it has helped change the social life of the country.
  Going to movie theaters can be very enjoyable, but sometimes it isn't a very pleasant experience. People have to stand in line to buy tickets, which might cost five dollars or more apiece. A few more dollars are spent on popcorn, candy, and drinks. Sometimes it's difficult to find good seats, and very often, the seats aren't very comfortable. In addition, there is always the possibility that a very tall person will sit down in front of the moviegoer and block the screen. It can also be very disturbing when people get up to go to the snack bar or bathroom in the middle of the film.
  The videocassette recorder (VCR) offers an alternative to a night at the movies. People can simply go to a "Video Club" store in their neighborhood, rent one or more movies for a day or a weekend, and watch them in the comfort of their own home. Videotapes can be rented at these special stores, as well as at many supermarkets, drug stores, and convenience stores. They aren't very expensive, just two dollars or so per day. Many different movies are available on videotape, from adventure movies and comedies to science fiction films and westerns.
  Watching a movie at home can be very convenient, and a lot cheaper. VCR owners can make their own popcorn and other snacks and sit back and enjoy a film with family and friends. They can stop the movie to make more snacks, answer the phone, or check on the baby. There are no lines to stand in, no tickets to buy, and no uncomfortable movie theater seats.
  For many people, however, enjoying a movie still means a night out at the neighborhood movie theater. For these moviegoers, nothing can replace the excitement of watching their favorite actors and actresses as they appear larger than life on a big movie screen. And for them, waiting in line, running to get good seats, and sitting with a huge box of popcorn while surrounded by other moviegoers is all part of the special movie theater experience that a VCR just can't match.

I. TRUE or FALSE? Put a T if the sentence is true, and F if it is false.

____ 1. VCRs have changed the way people in the U.S. watch movies.

____ 2. VCRs cost about two dollars.

____ 3. People like the convenience of VCRs.

____ 4. You can only rent videotapes from video clubs.

____ 5. Many people still prefer to go to movie theaters.

II. DID YOU UNDERSTAND? Circle the correct answer.

1. When people "disturb" you, they _____.
  a. bother you
  b. make you comfortable
  c. don't bother you at all

2. VCR owners appreciate the fact that _____.
  a. social life in the United States has changed
  b. VCRs can be rented
  c. videotapes can be stopped when it's necessary

3. An alternative to watching a videotape at home is _____.
  a. using a VCR
  b. watching a movie at a movie theater
  c. renting a videotape from a local video club

(continued)

4. A videocassette recorder is an example of _____.
   a. a video club
   b. the movie industry
   c. modern technology

5. The main idea of this reading passage is that _____.
   a. moviegoers prefer to watch movies in theaters
   b. VCRs have changed the way people in the U.S. watch movies
   c. most people in the U.S. have VCRs

CHECK-UP TEST: Chapters 7, 8, 9

A. Circle the correct answer.

Example _____ comes to $5.00.
    a. That'll
    (b.) That
    c. That's

1. I don't feel like _____.
    a. to go
    b. to going
    c. going

2. _____ I help you?
    a. May
    b. Do
    c. Would

3. How's he _____ his job?
    a. enjoying
    b. enjoy
    c. enjoys

4. Would you care for _____?
    a. seeing a movie
    b. to have a cup of coffee
    c. a drink

5. _____ it supposed to rain tomorrow?
    a. Won't
    b. Isn't
    c. Doesn't

6. _____ you decide is fine with me.
    a. That
    b. Whatever
    c. Would

7. We weren't aware _____.
    a. that
    b. them
    c. of that

8. Do you think you _____?
    a. coming
    b. could come
    c. to come

9. Can you tell me _____?
    a. where can I find a telephone
    b. where I can find a telephone
    c. where I find a telephone

10. How would you _____?
    a. care to have some more cake
    b. like having some more cake
    c. like to have some more cake

11. We _____ always come back later.
    a. could
    b. are
    c. supposed

B. Circle the best response for Speaker B.

Example   A. How about having a picnic?
    B. a. Have a nice day!
       (b.) That sounds like fun.
       c. I suppose it is.

1. A. How long will it take?
   B. a. About half an hour.
      b. About 10 inches.
      c. It's very short.

2. A. Why did you sign that book?
   B. a. It's my name.
      b. Because I sign it.
      c. It's mandatory.

3. A. Have you ever done this before?
   B. a. Yes, I had.
      b. No, never.
      c. After I've done it.

4. A. Is there anything I can get you?
   B. a. I see.
      b. No, thanks. Everything's fine.
      c. It doesn't matter to me.

5. A. Would you happen to know Sally?
   B. a. Yes, as a matter of fact.
      b. Sorry. I didn't know that.
      c. I suppose she is.

6. A. I don't feel like going there.
   B. a. Well, how about going to a movie?
      b. I've learned how.
      c. What a good suggestion.

7. A. Be sure you lock the car.
   B. a. I'm sure.
      b. I will.
      c. It's mandatory.

C. Write the correct word.

| around | down | for | in | of | off | on | out | together | up |

Example Take __off__ your jacket.

1. Are you going to participate _____ the contest?
2. Let's go _____ for dinner.
3. Who'll take care _____ the kids?
4. The children are putting _____ a jigsaw puzzle.
5. I always shop _____ before I make a big purchase.
6. Walk _____ these steps to the basement.
7. I have to work _____ my homework this weekend.
8. Don't forget to clean _____ your room!
9. Would you care _____ dessert?

D. Circle the correct word.

Example [I / **(I'm)**] afraid I can't.

1. [Are / Is] there anything else?
2. [I'm / I'd] like you to meet my friend.
3. [Are / Do] you have any ideas?
4. [She / She's] supposed to come early.
5. [I'll / I've] "got it down pat."
6. [It's / It] doesn't matter to me.
7. The food [is / are] wonderful!
8. [Do / Would] you like a Pepsi?
9. [He's / He'd] rather see a comedy.

E. Listen and decide what the person is talking about.

Example
    a. medicine
   (b.) a movie
    c. vacation plans

1. a. an actress
   b. a TV program
   c. a regulation

2. a. a money order
   b. a washing machine
   c. a new shirt

3. a. a salad
   b. clothes
   c. a party

4. a. an order
   b. airplane tickets
   c. the weather

5. a. a pond
   b. a hem
   c. a paycheck

6. a. cookies
   b. tea
   c. rice

7. a. a student
   b. a hotel
   c. a box

8. a. a refund
   b. a sweater
   c. employment

9. a. accident victims
   b. bank customers
   c. calculators

TAPE SCRIPTS FOR LISTENING EXERCISES

Page 2 Exercise D

Listen and circle the correct response.

1. Where is Miguel?
2. Who are you?
3. When did you move in?
4. Where are you going?
5. How's Janet?
6. Which apartment do you live in?
7. What are you majoring in?
8. My name is Mary.
9. How do you do?

Page 12 Exercise E

Listen to the sentence. Circle the appropriate response.

1. I got the raise I was hoping for!
2. My husband wrecked our car.
3. She broke up with her fiancé last week.
4. My wife got a big promotion.
5. Their apartment was robbed last night.
6. I'm really enjoying my classes.
7. I didn't pass my driver's test.
8. My wife had a baby last night!
9. He finally went to Greece on his vacation.

Page 16 Exercise M

Listen to the conversation. Circle the letter of the correct sentence.

1. A. Are you from Los Angeles?
   B. No, I'm from Denver.
2. A. What do you do?
   B. I'm a gym teacher.
3. A. I'm going to get a raise!
   B. Me, too!
4. A. I just passed my driver's test.
   B. Congratulations.
5. A. So, what's new?
   B. They plan to go on strike soon.
6. A. Is Fred going to quit?
   B. Not as far as I know.
7. A. What did you do in Cleveland?
   B. I went to college there.
8. A. Where are you from?
   B. I was born in New York and lived there until I finished high school.
9. A. What did you do in England?
   B. I was a journalist.
10. A. Do you have any children?
    B. Yes. I have a boy and a girl.

Page 19 Exercise C

Listen and complete the sentence.

1. My friend is living . . .
2. I put the cars . . .
3. Do you have any plans . . .
4. Did he stop . . .
5. Let's work . . .
6. Let's clean the kitchen . . .
7. Please . . .
8. Did you take him . . .
9. Do you know who . . .

Page 19 Exercise D

Listen to the conversation. Circle the correct word.

1. A. I'd like the number of David Yu.
   B. How do you spell that?
   A. Y-U
2. A. How do you spell Flanigan?
   B. F-L-A-N-I-G-A-N.
3. A. What street?
   B. Beech Road.
   A. B-E-E-C-H?
   B. Yes.
4. A. Can you spell that?
   B. Sure. W-I-T-T-L-E-R.
5. A. Just a moment. I'd better check the spelling . . . Yes, it's K-R-I-Z-I-C-K.
6. A. How do you spell Rio de Janeiro?
   B. R-I-O D-E J-A-N-E-I-R-O.
7. A. Did you say H-E-N-L-E-Y?
   B. Yes.
8. A. Do you spell Ramirez with a "z" or an "s"?
   B. A "z."

Page 21 Exercise G

Listen to the conversation. Circle the correct number.

1. A. I'd like the number of Bob Williams.
   B. Just a moment. The number is 539-7899.
2. A. Is this 592-8622?
   B. Yes, it is.
3. A. I guess I dialed the wrong number.
   B. What number did you dial?
   A. 832-5660.
4. A. Did you dial 860-5439?
   B. Yes, I did.

5. A. What's your telephone number?
   B. 834-5935.
6. A. Are you sure this is the correct number?
   B. Let me check. 648-2341. Yes, that's it!

Page 24 Exercise N

Listen to the announcement. Circle the words you hear.

1. The bus for Las Vegas is now leaving from gate thirteen.
2. Attention . . . passengers for New York and New Haven . . . your bus is at gate eleven.
3. Attention, passengers. The nine-thirty bus is now boarding at gate five.
4. Your attention, please. The three o'clock bus to Philadelphia is now boarding.
5. Attention please. The eleven forty-five bus to Kansas City is now leaving from gate seventeen.
6. Attention . . . passengers for San Francisco. Your bus is now boarding at gate twelve.
7. Passengers going to Chicago . . . Your bus will leave at ten thirty from gate two.
8. Your attention, please. The next bus to Baltimore will leave from gate eight.

Page 24 Exercise P

Listen and follow the directions to different places. Write the letter of the place the people are talking about in each conversation.

1. A. Could you please tell me how to get to the library?
   B. Okay. Walk down Fourth Street to Broad Street and turn left. Walk one block and you'll see the library on the corner of Third and Broad.
2. A. Can you tell me how to get to the laundromat?
   B. Sure. Walk down Oak Street to Third Street and make a right. You'll see the laundromat in the middle of the block.
3. A. How do I get to the zoo?
   B. Follow Fourth Street to Broad Street. Make a left on Broad Street and go three more blocks to First Street. You'll see the zoo on the left, at the intersection of First and Broad.
4. A. Do you know how to get to Max's Supermarket?
   B. Yes. Follow Fourth Street all the way to the end and make a left. Go one block and you'll see it on the left.
5. A. Could you possibly tell me how to get to River City High School?
   B. Uh-húh. Go down Fourth Street two blocks and make a left onto Broad Street. Go two more blocks and make a right on Second Street. You'll see the school on your right.
6. A. Excuse me. Is there a parking lot nearby?
   B. Yes. Follow Fourth Street all the way to the end. You'll see it on the left.
7. A. Where's City Hall?
   B. Follow Oak Street two blocks and make a right onto Second Street. Walk two more blocks. You'll see City Hall at the intersection of Broad and Second.
8. A. I'm looking for the bus station. Can you help me?
   B. Sure. Walk down Fourth Street to Main Street and make a left. Follow Main Street to Second Street. You'll see the bus station on the corner.
9. A. Do you by any chance know where the bank is?
   B. Yes. Go down Fourth to Main and make a left. Go two blocks and make a right. The bank's in the middle of the block on the right.

Page 26 Exercise S

Listen to the conversation. Did the person understand the directions? Circle *Yes* or *No*.

1. A. Take Exit 15.
   B. I'm following you.
2. A. Go north.
   B. Could you please repeat that?
3. A. Turn left at Second Avenue.
   B. I didn't get that.
4. A. Take the first right and you'll see a sign.
   B. I understand.
5. A. Go to the next corner and turn right.
   B. I didn't follow you.
6. A. Drive through 3 traffic lights and make a right.
   B. I'm with you.
7. A. Turn left at the light, go about a mile and you'll see a sign.
   B. I've got it.
8. A. Take the second left after the intersection.
   B. All right.

Page 29 Exercise F

Listen and circle the best response.

Example Where are you from?
1. What's new with you?
2. Have you got all that?
3. What are you going to do tonight?
4. Have a nice weekend!
5. How long do you plan to work here?
6. Could you repeat the last part?
7. When is the next flight to Chicago?
8. Why are you here?

Page 33 Exercise H

Listen and complete the sentence.

1. I need a dozen . . .
2. Could you pick up a quart of . . .
3. We have to get a bottle of . . .
4. Did you get a tube of . . .
5. Can you do me a favor and get a box of . . .
6. I've got to get a head of . . .
7. I need a stick of . . .
8. Could you buy a couple of . . .

Page 35 Exercise K

Listen to the sentence. Circle the correct answer.

1. Excuse me. Did you say Aisle 3?
2. Sorry. Did you say H Street?
3. Is this Aisle J?
4. You can find it in Aisle 8.
5. Do you spell that with a D?
6. I'm sorry. I said G.
7. We need fourteen.
8. Pardon me. Is this N Street?
9. What number is this? Seventy?
10. Sorry. Did you say F Street?

Page 36 Exercise N

Listen to each sentence. Circle the correct price.

1. That comes to thirteen dollars and fifteen cents.
2. The total is eighteen dollars and ten cents.
3. Your change is seven dollars and forty cents.
4. It's hard to believe how little you can buy for sixteen dollars and forty-three cents.
5. Fifteen dollars and seventy-six cents? That's unbelievable!
6. How about that! It's only thirty dollars and fifty-eight cents.
7. That'll be twenty-two dollars and eleven cents.
8. Nineteen dollars and eighty-eight cents, please.

Page 36 Exercise P

Listen to each sentence. Circle the correct word.

1. These aren't difficult to make.
2. It's really delicious!
3. I think it's really convenient.
4. It has a brand new kitchen.
5. It's very complicated.
6. It's within walking distance of school.

Page 45 Exercise O

Listen and circle the correct sentence.

1. He took lessons for five years.
2. She's been studying English for two years.
3. He was an architect.
4. She's been a computer analyst since college.
5. I've been working in the Accounting Department for a long time.
6. We lived in that apartment building for four years.
7. She was a receptionist until the office shut down.
8. They've been planning the meeting for a long time.

Page 50 Exercise B

Listen and circle the correct sentence.

1. Could you send an engine unit right away?
2. We need a repairman right away.
3. I think there's a robber in my neighbor's house.
4. She just fell down a flight of stairs.
5. Call the animal removal specialist right away.
6. The kitchen floor has flooded!
7. Please send an ambulance here right away!
8. There's been an accident at the intersection.
9. A dog has just been hit by a car.
10. Can you send a squad car?

Page 52 Exercise E

Listen to the conversation. Then listen to the sentence and circle *True* or *False*.

A. Police.
B. I want to report an accident.
A. Okay.
B. An airplane has landed on the expressway.
A. What's your name?
B. Rick Walters.
A. Where did this occur?
B. About two miles south of the airport near Exit 4.
A. Okay. We'll be there right away.

1. There was an accident at the airport.
2. Rick Walters called to report the accident.

Now listen to the next conversation.

A. Police.
B. I want to report a robbery.
A. Okay. Go ahead.
B. A drug store has just been robbed at Milford Shopping Mall.
A. What's your name?
B. Helen Nichols.

3. Helen Milford called to report a robbery.
4. Someone robbed a drug store.

Now listen to the next conversation.

A. Sergeant Garner.
B. I'd like to report a mugging.
A. Yes. Go on.
B. A man just mugged two women in front of my apartment building. The address is forty-two fifty-three Harrison Street.

5. Two women just mugged someone.
6. Sergeant Garner called to report the mugging.

Now listen to the next conversation.
- A. Police Department.
- B. There's been an accident on Highway 85. A patrol car has been hit by a bus.

7. A bus hit a police car.
8. An accident has just occurred on Highway 85.

Page 52   Exercise G

Listen to the sentence.   Circle the problem.

1. Can you suggest a good lotion?
2. I recommend this new decongestant spray.
3. I need a couple of aspirin.
4. It gets frizzy in this humidity.
5. Try these eyedrops.
6. I didn't sleep well last night.

Page 57   Exercise R

Listen to the directions.   Put the number under the correct bottle.

1. You have to take four tablets two times a day.
2. You're supposed to take two pills after eating.
3. You need to mix two teaspoons into orange juice at breakfast.
4. Don't forget: One capsule four times a day.
5. Remember to take one teaspoon twice a day.
6. You're supposed to take four tablespoons every day.

Page 61   Exercise E

Listen and circle the correct response.

Example Have you ever flown before?
1. Is Tuesday convenient for you?
2. Are you sure about that?
3. What was your last job?
4. How long have you been living here?
5. Do you have a benefits package?
6. Have you got all that?
7. Could you tell me a little more?
8. Could you do me a favor?
9. Are pets allowed?

Page 63   Exercise D

Listen to the conversation.   Which one are they talking about?

1. A. Which one are you interested in?
   B. The one with the 18-inch screen.
2. A. Which one would you like?
   B. The one that beeps every hour.
3. A. Which one would you like to buy?
   B. The one with two doors.
4. A. Which one would you like to try?
   B. The one with a manual transmission.
5. A. Which one should I take?
   B. The one with the benefits program.

6. A. Which one do you want?
   B. The one with the largest memory.
7. A. Which one should we purchase?
   B. The one with remote control.
8. A. Which one did you get?
   B. The self-cleaning one.

Page 65   Exercise G

Listen to the conversation.   Circle the words you hear.

1. A. I'm looking for a brown leather belt.
   B. What size?
   A. 34.
2. A. Do you know what size you are?
   B. Yes. I'm a 15 neck and a 33 sleeve.
   A. All right. One moment, please.
3. A. I'd like this skirt in a medium.
   B. Yes. Here we are.
4. A. I usually wear a size 7.
   B. Here. Try this in a small.
5. A. I'll take this brown one.
   B. Okay. Will this be cash or charge?
6. A. I'd like to buy a blue permanent press blouse.
   B. What size?
   A. Twelve, I think.
7. A. I want to buy a beige belt . . . size 32.
   B. All right. Let's look on that rack over there.
8. Do you have this shirt in a permanent press?

Page 66   Exercise J

Listen and circle the best answer.

1. Could you carry this box for me?
2. This recipe is simple.
3. We need a larger rug.
4. These earrings are too tight.
5. This tie is too conservative!
6. It's too short!
7. Hmm. This brown belt is too dark.
8. This blouse is too simple.

Page 67   Exercise N

Listen and circle the correct number.

1. A. How long will it take?
   B. It'll take about ten days.
2. A. How much will it cost?
   B. It'll be twelve dollars and ninety-six cents.
3. A. How much does it weigh?
   B. It's eleven pounds.
4. A. What's the cost?
   B. Fourteen sixty-eight.
5. A. When will it get there?
   B. It'll get there in about nine days.

6. A. How heavy is it?
   B. Four pounds.
7. A. How much will that be?
   B. It'll be thirteen seventy-eight.
8. A. How much do I owe you?
   B. Twelve sixty-four.

Page 72   Exercise G

Listen and decide what they're talking about. Circle the best answer.

1. A. Could you tell me how to take it out?
   B. Sure. First, flip the switch to turn it off. Then twist it to the left and it'll come out.
   A. Thanks.
2. A. Can you tell me what to do?
   B. Certainly. Put your paper in. Press this key for the left margin and this key for the right.
   A. Thank you very much.
3. A. Do you think you'd be able to tell me how?
   B. I'd be happy to. Lift up the old spool like this. Then put the new one on the spindle and flip this switch.
   A. Thanks very much.
4. A. Could I possibly ask you to help?
   B. I'd be glad to. Take out the empty tank. Then attach the hoses to the new tank.
   A. Thanks.
5. A. Do you think you could tell me how?
   B. Sure. Put the caller on "hold." Dial the extension. When they answer, tell them they have a call and hang up.
   A. Okay. Thank you.
6. A. Do you think you could show me how?
   B. Certainly. Press this button to turn it on. Put the cassette in here. Press the start button.
   A. Thanks!

Page 87   Exercise G

Listen to the weather forecast and circle the sentence that is true.

1. Here's today's weather forecast for the metropolitan area: We're going to have rain this afternoon. Temperatures will be in the low eighties.
2. Here is the weather update for our area: We have a sunny day ahead. The present temperature is forty-five degrees. Tonight's low will be in the thirties.
3. A. And now, let's hear the weather report from Jim Reed.
   B. Thank you, Jane. It looks like we'll have a little snow this morning . . . but nothing to worry about. And put on those heavy jackets! Today's high will only be about twenty-five.
4. It's going to be a hot, muggy evening with temperatures in the mid eighties. We have a seventy percent chance of thunderstorms throughout the night.
5. Now here's our latest weather update from the Rockin' Ninety-Nine Weather Center. The good news is NO MORE RAIN in the forecast. We'll have clearing tonight, but watch out for the fog early tomorrow morning while you're driving to work.
6. A. Now it's time to hear from our weatherman, Bob Wilson. Bob, what's it look like out there today?
   B. Well, Joe, hold on to your hat! We're in for a windy day with gusts up to twenty miles per hour.

Page 89   Exercise M

Listen and circle the correct response.

1. What would you like to drink?
2. Would you prefer salad or soup with that?
3. I'll have a glass of wine.
4. What would you care for?
5. I'd rather have tofu.
6. That's spaghetti, a salad with Italian dressing, and a glass of wine.

Page 90   Exercise Q

Listen and complete the sentence.

1. We don't know how . . .
2. Would you care for some rice . . .
3. Your size . . .
4. These shops . . .
5. How much does the seat . . .
6. Would you care . . .
7. Are these jeans . . .
8. Peas . . .
9. I wrecked . . .
10. Which features . . .

Page 91   Exercise R

Listen and circle the correct answer.

1. A. I can give you two seats in the bleachers.
   B. How much are they?
   A. Three dollars each.
   B. Okay.
2. A. I'd like five tickets in the grandstand for today's match.
   B. Sorry. The grandstand is sold out.
3. A. How much would three tickets cost?
   B. They're two dollars apiece. So that'll be six dollars.
4. There aren't any seats left for tonight's concert.
5. A. What seats do you have available?
   B. I can give you two seats in Section G.

6. A. How much would they be?
   B. Ten dollars each.
   A. Okay. I'll take two of them.

7. A. I'll take four seats on the ground level.
   B. Sorry. We only have the upper level.

8. The matinee's sold out, so I bought tickets for tonight's performance.

Page 91   Exercise T

What movies are playing? Call the movie theater and listen to the recordings. Listen to the first recording. Then answer these questions.

> The State Theater is proud to present *One Last Kiss*. There are shows this evening at seven-thirty and nine-thirty. Tickets are four dollars apiece.

Listen to the second recording. Then answer these questions.

> Thank you for calling the Town Theater. We are happy to be showing the popular film, *The Friendly Giant*. The matinee show is at one o'clock. Other shows are at three o'clock and five o'clock. Tickets for the matinee are three dollars. All other shows are six dollars each.

Page 97   Exercise E

Listen and decide what the person is talking about.

Example   I feel like seeing a western.
1. It's mandatory.
2. Could you please tell me how to turn this on?
3. I'll have Italian dressing on it.
4. Is that for here or to go?
5. Why are there so many deductions?
6. Would you care for a few more?
7. How about sending it first class?
8. Do you think your wife will like this one?
9. Let me see if they're in stock.